Cover illustration: Whilst fire destroys, it also brings new life to forests and heathlands. Here at Anglesea on Victoria's south coast, *Xanthorrhoea australis*, an ancient member of the lily family, is initiated into full flower. The sparse new canopy of the Eucalyptus in the background illustrates too their recuperative powers

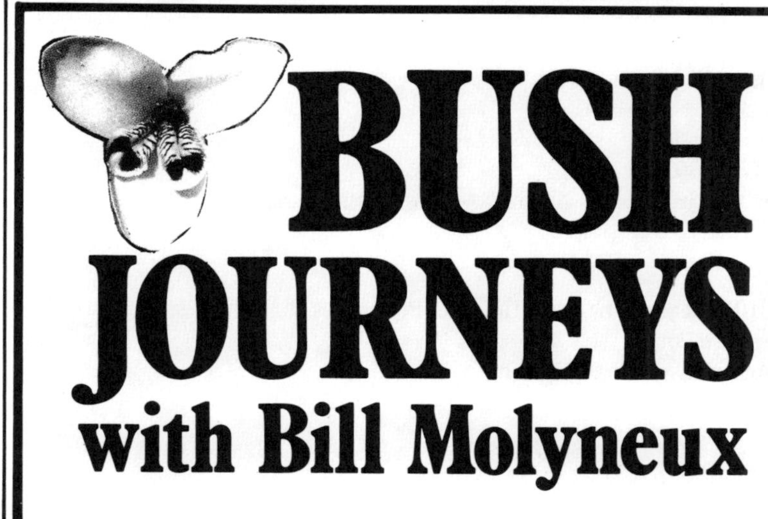

Nelson

First published in Australia in 1985 by
Thomas Nelson Australia
480 La Trobe Street, Melbourne Victoria 3000

National Library of Australia
Cataloguing in Publication data:
Molyneux, Bill.
Bush journeys.
ISBN 0 17 006656 8.
1. Botany — Australia. 2. Australia — Description and travel. I. Title.
518′.0994

Typeset in 11/13 Clearface by Trade Graphics Pty. Ltd.
Designed by Sarn Potter
Printed in Australia by Impact Printing

CONTENTS

Dedication

Abide quietly with it,
and the land will share with you
the secrets of its rhythm.

Care not for it,
but only for what you may take from it,
and the rhythm
will falter and die.

With this, I dedicate *Bush Journeys* to those dear and near, who most clearly share its implied message: Sue, for love, companionship and a joy for giving without expectation of reward; Diana and Brian, for friendship and encouragement; Judy and Clyde, who share the knowledge of the earth's rhythm with those people to whom it means most: the Aborigines.

1 EARLY ADVENTURES & BEYOND

My early adventures, as distinct from journeys, were partly in the disused bluestone quarries that pock-marked the landscape around my Footscray home. These cavernous, sheer-walled chasms presented a challenge and provided an educational experience. Later they became the repositories of western suburbs garbage, and a major hunting ground for that great little hunting dog, the fox-terrier, bred to capture the hordes of rats that multiplied in the rubbish. With adventurous friends, clinging by fingernail and toehold, I would move across the black perpendicular faces in search of birds' nests. We had no fear, and we gained confidence in our young bodies and one another. It was my first experience of sharing adventure, and of team spirit.

Often, during an exceptionally wet winter, there would be so much water in the quarries that we needed to construct makeshift rafts to approach our favoured climbing spots. These boat trips were often interrupted while we examined frog spawn caught amongst box thorn, or later, collected the tadpoles when they had hatched. We would take some of these home in a jar, to witness the magical process of their changing before our eyes into frogs, completing the cycle. But where had the frogs come from in the beginning?

During the summer the floors of the quarries were like ovens, the soil so parched that great cracks appeared in it. Crickets in plague proportions lived in these cracks, and under every rock or piece of rusty sheet iron. But deep down in those cracks sufficient moisture remained for frogs to live in a dormant state. Here they stayed until the next season's rain flooded their crannies, bringing them out of their hibernation to begin the magical cycle again. It is not only amphibians such as frogs which undergo periods of dormancy; but as well, plants which are either blanketed by winter's snow, in our alpine areas, or scorched by searing sun and parched for rain, do likewise.

When I grew beyond birds' nests and frogs at this level I took to riding my bike to more distant fields of adventure. Where suburbs now spread almost uninterrupted from Footscray to Melton, there used to be miles of open basalt plains. Down through this hard rock, rivers and creeks have slowly cut and shaped their courses. With my long-ago friends, Ken, Lindsay, Colin and Keith, pushing across the open plains to these rivers was the supreme adventure.

Where towering brick housing blocks now reflect in the less than pristine waters of the Maribyrnong River, we used to fish, swim, or lie silently on our stomachs watching the platypuses sunning themselves on the surface in the late afternoon light. At night we fished for and invariably caught eels, the contortionist 'slimies', which knitted half our fishing lines into inextricable knots before we could remove them from the hooks. Not then the coloured scree of household rubbish tumbling down and blowing across the steep slopes to the water's edge.

When I was only ten or eleven Sherbrooke and its forests was a natural classroom. Either on holidays (a big adventure from Footscray in those days) or on a day trip by tram, train, bus and foot, my father and I would walk these shaded tracks, scrambling down steep gullies and climbing up through ferns and tall trunks. To a small boy this was a world with no end, its boundaries so distant you would surely perish before finding your way out of the moist gloom. Stalking lyrebirds was our great joy, and to this day I have not seen another animal or bird display to equal a male lyrebird in full dance and song. Now, I can wander only ten minutes from my backdoor and still derive as much pleasure in distinguishing the pure mimicry of a lyrebird from the birds it is imitating.

We would drop into gullies and measure the gigantic buttresses of *Eucalyptus regnans*, the tallest hardwood on earth. Craning our heads back, we would become dizzy watching the clouds scud across the very tips of these giants, hundreds of feet above us.

It was on one of our quiet walks that we met a gentle, bespectacled man who informed us that he was looking for a small marsupial mouse with the wonderful name of *Sminthopsis crassicaudata*. To a ten-year-old this was very impressive, and the name immediately became embedded in my memory — even if later it did turn out to be another species which inhabited these wet forests. What a joy it was also to find that this quiet man was Phillip Crosbie Morrison, whose natural history radio programme I listened to every week. I did not meet him again; but in 1975, when I was living in Merrimu, the original Sherbrooke house, I found from notes in old books that that was where Crosbie Morrison had stayed. Memories of that earlier meeting and my own adventures in that beautiful forest flooded back whenever I walked through there as I often did when I lived beside it.

Childhood impressions, both good and bad, are very strong; even though my eye is now much more experienced, I still observe my natural surroundings as I learned to do with such people. I now know that the die for my future interest and commitment was firmly cast during that early Sherbrooke experience. School, sport and social involvement came and went before I spent any length of time again in constant contact with rivers and bushland.

After an uninspiring involvement with secondary education, I found myself jackarooing in the Riverina, that broad-plains country of south New South Wales. Over a period of four years I worked near such romantic waterways as the Murrumbidgee, Murray, and Darling rivers, the Yanco and Billabong creeks. These were bordered by *Eucalyptus camaldulensis*, the ubiquitous tree of most of Australia's internal waterways, and *Eucalyptus largiflorens*, the black box of flooded low areas. I have seen these rivers and creeks hardly running one year, and the next year becoming continuous sheets of water 30 kilometres wide, their individual courses hardly discernible. I have canoed on Lake Urana where there were so many water birds that you felt that the whole of the populations of those species must surely be there at once. Two years later I walked across the same basin during a drought, and felt that some destructive force had wiped out all that I had previously seen.

Such were the early experiences and observations that led to my later understanding of the dramatic changes this wonderful land can undergo. And of course I found that those birds hadn't disappeared from the face of the earth, but were happily occupying a tract of water somewhere else.

I find it sad that relatively few people have any real knowledge or understanding of our diverse natural environment; some are simply not interested. With my greater understanding of the history of the shaping of this land, I fear for its future security. Too often it is the insensitive and the ignorant who control the development or 'improvement' of forest or heathland. The sins of many an ill-conceived plan have been visited upon us many times. Massive erosion, wind strip of top soil, and vast salination, have already been devastating. Our learning processes would seem to be slow, and the same mistakes are made again and again.

While, on occasions, I have undertaken and enjoyed solitary journeys to bushland areas both far off and closer at hand, it is when I share these experiences with others that I find greatest pleasure and understanding. Where I go, and what I see there, is more precisely observed and understood with more than one set of eyes, and I know that my observation is enhanced at all levels.

My earlier intensive interest, which centred on finding out as much as possible about the genus *Grevillea*, necessitated travelling far and wide across Australia to track down species, often in isolated localities. I was accompanied on many of these early trips by my former wife and three small children, who were often woken very early on Sunday mornings to undertake a long day's search somewhere in Victoria. Our greatest adventure as a family was to travel across the Nullarbor to Western Australia one summer in the mid-1960s. The rigors of the old dirt road and its cavernous potholes, shortage of water, excessive heat, and the trial to three children under ten of setting up and dismantling camp every day, were forgotten in the magical experiences encountered.

The sheer isolation of camping in the middle of the Nullarbor was awe inspiring and our link with, and dependence on favourable treatment by the elements was inescapable. It was on this lonely plain that we experienced a phenomenon not seen by us before or since, one probably caused by an atmospheric aberration. It was an evening of crystal clarity, and as the full array of stars dotted the sky, they did so in dimensional layers. As we lay in our sleeping bags in the open, we felt we would only need to reach above us to pluck a jewel from the heavens. Layer upon layer of stars shone above us, till they were so distant, as to be scarcely discernable specks.

At another time and place, I sat with Sue and my two sons within touching distance of two mating tiger snakes. We had chanced upon this pair standing upright with their bodies coiled together and just the end few centimetres of their tails on the ground. They were oblivious to our presence for many minutes, and it was only when one, becoming aware of us, struck the other with its head with blurred rapidity, that the spell was broken, and they slid away.

Even now, though my children have long ago left the sphere of my influence, on the brief occasions when we do meet and talk, it is obvious that they still retain a sense of wonder and inquisitiveness about the natural world.

I am fortunate that in the last decade or so I have shared so many experiences with Sue Forrester, and we have introduced one another to, or discovered together, some magical places. The feelings of awe and spirituality which pervaded my senses in the Kimberleys, have for me never been equalled by any man-made place of worship. One wonders if there is some magical force guiding one on a long path of observing and learning; almost like a child's game, where one moves from one secret place to the next, seeking out and comprehending the clues left there.

I consider it a privilege to share some of my very personal and enlightening experiences with whoever may read them. I know that there is no end to the paths of *Bush Journeys* for me; I will walk them all my life, observing, learning and then sharing. My hope is that there will always be places of solitude and isolation for those who, like Sue and I, rather than passing through, stop to partake of the communion with nature. Join me now as I recall some of our bush journeys, and share with us the experiences and understanding which we have derived from them.

Sue and Bill: breakfast on the Nullarbor

2 LITTLE DESERT

WESTERN VICTORIA

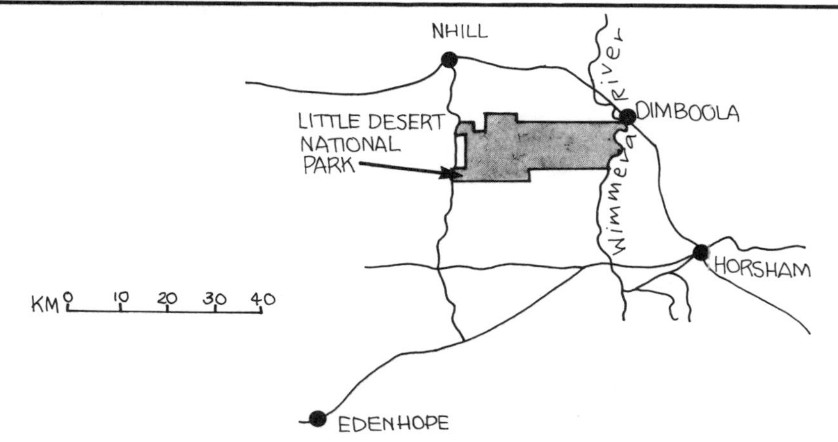

In the early days of my search for new plant knowledge the Little Desert, and to a lesser extent the Big Desert country, were areas in which I made new discoveries. We would set off from Melbourne at 5 p.m. on a Friday to spend two days somewhere in this drier western section of Victoria. Many trips centred on the Lowan Sanctuary at Kiata, situated in the northern section of the Little Desert National Park where the famed pair of lowan or mallee fowl, Romeo and Juliet, were in residence. Kiata is between Dimboola and Nhill in Western Victoria, and about 225 kilometres north-west of the Grampians as the crow flies. Invariably it was near to 1 a.m. before all were bedded down in their tents at the original camp site, and hardly, it seemed, were we asleep when we heard the cheery voice of Keith Hately going about his work as Ranger. Keith – who has long since retired as Ranger of the sanctuary, but is still actively interested in the birds – would always suggest a trip to the mallee fowl incubation mounds.

Apart from a stint during World War II, Keith has spent a lifetime of involvement in this often dry, hot environment. With his understanding of the birds and insects (with a specific interest in butterflies) as well as the plants of this area, he is a highly regarded natural historian.

The lowans constructed their mounds in clearings among mallee heath communities, and here the mound was set among *Eucalyptus incrassata, E. gracilis, Baeckea behrii,* and *Melaleuca uncinata* thickets. The under storey was partly comprised of *Lasiopetalum behrii,* a fine dainty leaved shrub with pink flowers, *Acacia glandulicarpa, Astroloma humifusum,* the 'cranberry heath', and *A conostephioides,* 'flame heath', popular food for emus. The small-leaved *Daviesia, D. brevifolia,* with open pink pea flowers, and the taller suckering form of *Grevillea aquifolium*, were also present, but possibly the most important plant in this community is *Acacia rigens*; for it is on the seed of this plant that the mallee fowl depends so much for food in summer time. It has been said that the amount of flowering and, through that, the quantity of available seed determine the number of eggs incubated. I have seen lowans feeding on dispersed acacia seed on coastal headlands, in Mid Mount Barren in southern Western Australia, and it is probable that similar controls on breeding are determined here by the supply of food.

Keith Hately and a lowan fowl

I recall vividly the first time I squatted silently a short distance from the nesting mound of a fowl. Having never previously seen the bird, I had visions, from the pile of sand and vegetation in front of me, of something much larger than the speckled fawn bird that silently appeared in response to Keith's call. It was the male, and he was not much larger than a domestic fowl, dwarfed by the metre-high mound he now mounted.

The clutch of eggs is buried in the mound, and the rotting vegetation provides the heat for the incubation supplied by body heat in most other birds. As we watched, the female now joined her companion, but stayed at the base of the mound. The male was scratching at the surface of the mound and occasionally inserting its beak into it. This is its way of determining the temperature level. If it finds this too high, it scratches back some of the cover to allow heat to escape; if it is too cool, then more sand and bush litter are applied.

When the chicks hatch, they fight their way upwards to light and air and join their parents. Doubtless since that first occasion twenty years ago, there have been new Romeos and Juliets; but I would not doubt that Keith has developed, with successive pairs, the gentle, trusting relationship he had with their ancestors.

From the original camping area (a more modern site is now in existence), dominated by the white trunks of *Eucalyptus leucoxylon*, a favourite trip was south toward Salt Lake. On the way a stop was invariably made at the windmill, which supplied a small dam of about 250 square metres. What makes this spot so interesting is its use, both at first light and at sunset, as a watering hole for kangaroos, emus, and a host of small birds. Finches, parrots, wrens and flycatchers could be seen together frequently, either drinking or chasing the insects that appeared in clouds. It was an oasis indeed, its lushness contrasting strangely with the dry lateritic sands above on the main south track.

A whole new range of plants to those seen previously around the camp site is to be found growing amongst the ferrous-coloured marbles of laterite. The one that seems to dominate this landscape, is a casuarina or 'she-oak'. This species, dwarf in habit, has a fine grey to blue-grey appearance, and is now known as *Allocasuarina muellerana*. It seemed to prefer flat platforms of ironstone with little soil cover.

Close by, and dominating its own shelf, was a dwarf 'mint bush', *Prostanthera aspalathoides*. Unlike the familiar blue or mauve 'mints' which are around 1.5-2 metres tall, this species, like many from dry areas, is small in both stature and foliage. The tiny clustered leaves are strongly aromatic, not minty, but with a more exotic pungent fragrance. The tubular flowers can be found as yellow, orange or red, growing in the one population. Because of the intensity of the colour and the small stature of the plants it is the floral display that is noticed. When not in flower the plant can easily be missed amongst other plants of similarly fine foliage.

A widespread plant, *Grevillea rosmarinifolia*, has its western limits in the Little Desert, and here it grows in association with plants found with it elsewhere. This form of *Grevillea rosmarinifolia*, which is also known as *G. glabella*, has fine needle foliage and waxy pink flowers. Forms in other parts of the state have red or yellow flowers.

Banksia marginata, with its yellow, often highly perfumed brush flowers, is a compact shrub in this sandy environment whereas, not far away in moister parts of the Grampians, it is a tall shrub of 3 or more metres. *Correa reflexa* is low and spreading, and its fine foliage, much reduced in comparison to other forms, gives an open appearance to this red-flowered specimen.

As you drop down a sandy track from this interesting stony area, and just before you take the final descent to Salt Lake, one of the rarer plants in it may be seen. This is *Calectasia cyanea*, 'blue tinsel lily', a small plant with fine stem-clasping sheathing leaves and shiny blue star flowers with yellow centres. This is an ancient plant which, as well as being widespread in western sandy parts of Victoria, and in South Australia, is found in similar habitats in Western Australia. Here it is often a companion to *Anigozanthos pulcherrimus*, 'golden kangaroo paw', and *Macropidia fuliginosa*, the 'black kangaroo paw', both of which are confined to Western Australia; and to a number of *Banksia* species. In the Little Desert it is associated with *Banksia ornata*, which is a small to medium shrub with yellow or orange brushes, and is confined to the western part of the state. It is also common in South Australia as far as Kangaroo Island. So while the plant species with which *Calectasia* grows differ, the community type and site requirements are similar.

Around the perimeter of Salt Lake grow large specimens of *Eucalyptus leucoxylon* var. *leucoxylon*, mostly a tall white-trunked tree with a pendulous canopy. There is a definite demarcation line as you drop into the lake floor, and the salt levels preclude all but very salt-tolerant plants. Even then the dominant plant, *Melaleuca halmaturorum*, a dense, small foliaged mounding large shrub, found mostly around salt areas, has a line beyond which it, too, seems unable to grow. This white-trunked plant replaces the similar *Melaleuca lanceolata*, which grows in clay loams free of excessive salt. *M. lanceolata* is transcontinental and is commonly found on coastal dunes, as it is in Victoria. In Western Australia it is the dominant large plant on Rottnest Island, and is known locally as the 'Rottnest tea-tree'.

Chenopods are the plants that can tolerate heavy salt conditions, having developed the ability to absorb large amounts of salt in a dilute state in their water uptake. When the salt levels in their turgid leaves become too high, they simply pass the salt out through pores, where it crystallises and is eventually washed or blown off. The common species found on salt lakes is *Kochia erioclada*, and I have even had it for company at frequent camp sites when travelling across the Nullarbor. While it is recognisable by its inflated grey leaves, it is the perianths with their flanged, coloured collars, that are the outstanding part of the plant. In different species of *Kochia*, they are red, pink, purple, green or orange, and are the obvious means of recognition.

Salt pans are the remnants of the seas that covered this country in past geological times. These ephemeral lakes are the lowest point of drainage systems, and seldom receive sufficient rainfall to carry fresh water. Salt and clay are leached out of the surrounding country and settle in these basins. As water evaporates, salt, clay and often gypsum form crusts which can be dazzlingly reflective and bakingly hot during the height of summer. At the Raak Plain, farther north in the Sunset Country, the gypsum is in such quantities that it is mined.

Lonely settlers may have found little in the Little Desert and mallee generally to enthuse about, so totally different must it have been from the cooler, greener pastures of the northern hemisphere. It is interesting that so few written records exist of how they viewed this land. By the way in which much of it was totally razed, they may have felt that God had made a dreadful mistake, and it was their duty to correct this. One can imagine the settler standing at his homestead, turning and looking to all points of the compass and seeing only bare sandy tracts stretching beyond the curve of the earth.

No doubt the conveniences of modern living and urban dwelling allow those of us who wish to gain pleasure from the surviving areas different perspectives. While we can lazily enjoy the pink and grey of a wheeling, screeching flock of galahs, nearby wheat farmers are planning ways to prevent them decimating the ripening crops. Likewise we see poetry in the movement of a bounding flock of kangaroo or a loping mob of emu, with their bouncing mops of feathers, rather than destroyers of fences or tramplers of crops.

With man's needs for land use increasing, a further imbalance of animals and birds will inevitably occur.

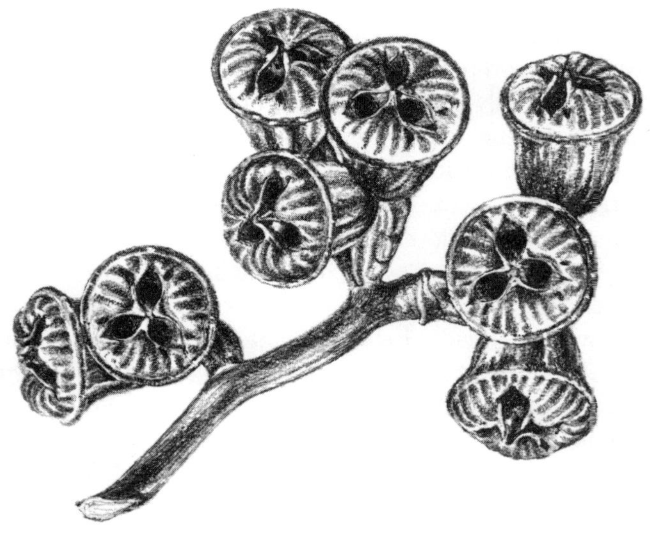

Eucalyptus burdettiana

3 MT STRADBROKE

VICTORIA

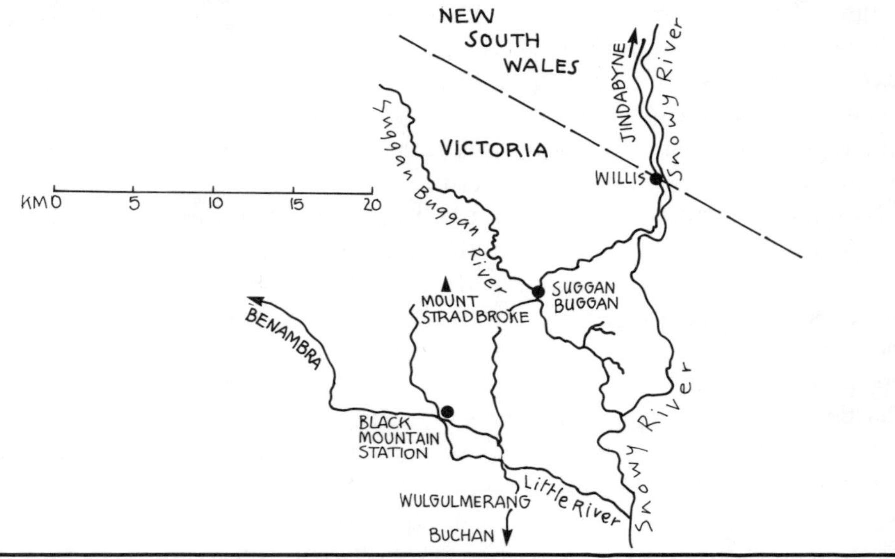

West of the Snowy River and some 12 kilometres (as the crow flies) south of the New South Wales border is the tiny settlement of Suggan Buggan. Just south of here is Black Mountain, a property on which pastoralist and naturalist Keith Rogers lived for many years. Acutely aware of the flora of the vast ranges and gorges surrounding his property, he used to accompany the noted naturalist Norman Wakefield on numerous trips, and he introduced him to the remote Reedy Creek Chasm and the plateau through which it cut, still as wild and difficult of access as when they explored it twenty-five years ago in 1960.

Keith Rogers was always eager, when he could spare the time, to accompany botanists to remote, unexplored areas, and it is thanks to him that many new records and discoveries have been made. I was fortunate enough to meet him and stay with him at Black Mountain in the last years before he moved to Bairnsdale. Like many men who have spent a lot of time on their own, he was shy and quiet, with a dry sense of humour. He never paraded his knowledge.

I had arranged with Keith to take a botanist colleague and myself to the north-east slopes of Mt Stradbroke, approximately 7 kilometres due north of his property. Here, on the steep upper slopes, we would be looking at a rare *Grevillea* which for many decades had been mistaken for *G. ramosissima*. That species is now known to grow in Victoria only on Pine Mountain near Corryong, although it is common throughout the tablelands of New South Wales. Unfortunately, owing to unexpected farm demands, Keith was not able to lead our trip; but he gave us clear instructions as to first getting to the summit of Stradbroke and then locating the correct slope.

With a compass bearing of north from the homestead, we set out towards the first lower slopes which obscured the main mountain. Once clear of fences, we made steady progress and entered the lower forests of *Eucalyptus rubida*, with its clear trunk, and *E. radiata* ssp. *robertsonii*, lightly barked almost all over and emitting a strong peppermint smell from its leaves. On the creeks and the swamps in these lower areas was a more localised species, *E. camphora*, which is confined to these moist, cooler parts of Victoria and New South Wales. It is mainly clean-trunked but has some bark at its base, and ribbon-like bark shedding from farther up the trunk.

On the banks of the creeks, tributaries of Little River which flows through the Rogers property on its way to the Snowy River, grew a tall, shrubby form of *Grevillea lanigera*, the 'woolly grevillea'. This pink and white flowered shrub has a wide range of habitats from moist to dry subalpine areas, through to coastal headlands. *Gaultheria appressa*, one of Australia's few members of the erica family, is a common shrub that grows as low hummocks throughout the tussock grass. This shiny-leaved shrub has small flowers, followed by masses of soft waxy white to pink berries.

Near by in moister boggy areas is an unusual member of the epacrid family, *Richea continentis*, the only species in Victoria. It is erect, with stiff stem-clasping leaves, and is often nearly a metre tall. The cream flowers are in dense terminal spikes. Richeas are more a part of the Tasmanian landscape where a number of species occur; *R. continentis* is found only in the south-eastern part of the mainland.

We gradually climbed through pleasant grassed glades, amongst small forms of *Acacia mearnsii* in full flower. This pinnate leaved wattle is one of the later flowering species and is a structurally dominant plant of montane forests.

We now entered the first stands of the forest form of *Eucalyptus pauciflora*, the snow gum, more familiar to most people in its stunted form above the snowline. No stunted dwarfs this lot: they were at least 30 metres tall, and it was only by searching beneath the trees for discarded seed capsules that a positive identification could be made. This white-trunked tree, although generally found in alpine or subalpine habitats, has an unusually disjointed distribution in Victoria, being found on the Mornington Peninsula and in the very south-west of the state. What an interesting tale of evolution and adaptation that would be, if it were unravelled!

It was just after entering the stands of snow gums, and not far below the summit, that we suddenly came into a broad open grassed area without trees. I noticed a movement among the trees on the far side about 30 metres away, and suddenly a white stallion with three mares behind him broke into the clearing. The stallion quickly herded the mares back into the timber and came galloping back across the clearing towards us. We were close enough to timber to run behind it if we needed to, but he stopped about 6 metres in front of us, snorted, reared on his hind legs; then, dropping back to the ground, he turned to join his mares and disappeared into the trees.

This country carries large numbers of brumbies, and dingoes, too. On another occasion I sat with Sue and watched a fawn male dingo playing with his multi-coloured pups for some time before he realised we were present and led them into cover. It is not unusual for a lone male dingo to entice farm bitches to join him, thereby often producing black and tan offspring.

We saw no further sign of the horses, and within a few minutes broke into open ground which led to the rocky summit of Mt Stradbroke. A plant we had not previously seen during the day dominated the broken ground below the summit; it was a 'mint bush', *Prostanthera phylicifolia*, a shrub of no more than 60 centimetres in this exposed position. It did not have traditional 'mint bush' leaves, the leaves being narrow and shiny, and the flowers, a number of which still persisted on plants, were white with yellow blotched throats. It was my first encounter with this attractive plant, which is confined, in Victoria, to eastern Gippsland, but also occurs in northern states on this side of the continent.

The view from the summit cairn was spectacular, the Snowy Mountains dominating the northern horizon, with the Cobberas below them to the south-west, just within Victoria. Our route down the opposite side was easy to find when, in mid-afternoon, we started our descent. It was steep and often over wet shelves where moisture seeped out of the rock. On one of these shelves, where a reasonable depth of soil had accumulated, *Micromyrtus ciliata* was growing.

Unlike the *Prostanthera*, this small myrtle, with fine aromatic leaves, can be found in the most diverse habitats throughout Victoria. The extreme opposite to this population is that one on the far side of the state growing on mallee sand hills. In between, it occupies a range of country including the Grampians, the whipstick country north of Bendigo, and the granite country near Beechworth. Though it is currently the only recognised species in Victoria, there are around ten in Western Australia.

After crossing another steep broad rock face, we found ourselves in a dense copse of mallee eucalypts. By the distinctive buds, I took it for a dwarf form of *Eucalyptus glaucescens*, which can be a medium-sized, mostly clear-barked tree of lower altitudes. It had fine 'clothes-prop' stems and long pendulous leaves, and capped buds and fruits in groups of three. This is the only place where I have encountered this interesting small tree, which has now been given its own specific title *E. saxatilis*. The name roughly translates to 'of rocky places', an appropriate epithet considering its habitat.

We had dropped a considerable distance from the summit, and after emerging from the mallee we paused to survey the eastern country below us which led to the Snowy River. Directly below we could detect where the Suggan Buggan River, which starts on the east side of the Cobberas, cut an undulating eastward path.

One of the phenomena of this area could be seen even from this height by its sombre colour, which stood out from the eucalyptus canopy. This tree, *Callitris columellaris*, is normally found in drier inland areas and is a strong component of these upper Snowy River woodlands. This part of the range has often been referred to as a rain shadow area, indicating lower precipitation than is the norm for the surrounding country; but I don't know if this fully explains the presence of this widespread native pine.

The often glaucous foliage of *Eucalyptus albens*, 'white box', could also be seen against the contrast of greener foliage, and it too has a disjunct limited occurrence in this part of the state. Normally it is found in the drier northern parts of Victoria and central slopes of New South Wales. It is a shapely tree, with a rounded crown and, like many of the 'box' group, it makes an ideal shelter tree for stock. From a distance it looks white all over, hence the specific name; but its bark is light grey and flaky, and the general white appearance is imparted by the waxy covering on the buds and small branches.

We had to drop a further 150 metres or thereabouts before we were to find the *Grevillea* we sought, on a broad shelf, and on lower gentler slopes. It was growing as a dense community, and even in early December, numerous terminal and horizontal racemes of white flowers were attracting flocks of honeyeating birds and bees. The foliage of this species (currently an affinity to the recently named *Grevillea willisii*) is deeply lobed and stiff, while the undersurfaces are often felted white, as are the young stems.

I mentally compared this plant with *Grevillea willisii*, whose main location is in the area where Bundara River enters the Mitta River north-west of Omeo. That

is a more robust plant, with less deeply divided leaves, but still exhibiting the prominent flowers thrust out at the ends of branches. These could hardly be missed by the birds, which alight on the almost horizontal stems to probe deeply into the individual flowers for nectar. It is a marvellous example of adaptation and interdependence. On a later occasion, Sue and I were able to compare this with a third, and equally interesting form of the variable *Grevillea willisii*. This occurs on dry, rocky slopes deep in the Reedy River gorge, which cuts deeply into the Nunniong Plateau. This remote area is roughly midway between the other two occurrences, and is a harsh, dry environment which can become stiflingly hot in summer. Sue and I had spent time investigating this pristine narrow gorge, and at the day's end were climbing out up a steep incline. About 100 metres above the river, we came to an outcrop of large broken rock, which we had to negotiate. Growing around its base was a grevillea no more than half a metre in height, but with an extensive spread.

I recognised the leaves as being similar to those of *Grevillea willisii*; but, like the habit, they were much reduced in size as a response to this tough environment. The other adaptation was also interesting, in that the flower spikes were pendulous and almost hidden within the tangle of rigid stems and leaves. As they aged they turned a bright pink, which meant the racemes were bicolorous. We wondered whether this further adaptation was to prevent desiccation by the atmospheric heat radiating from the rocks; and, if honeyeating birds were the pollinating agents, whether in the shaded cover the pink flowers indicated aged (and therefore less productive) flowers than the white. As my mind returned to Mt Stradbroke and its collection of flowering and seeding specimens, I again wondered at the forces that still move, mostly imperceptibly, in bringing about such adaptations as they have for millions of years.

But back to Mt Stradbroke. The sun had long disappeared behind the mountains above us; and even though I was loath to leave this remote slope with its broad eastern vistas we realised that not many hours of daylight remained. It was a further two hours before we again reached the summit of Mt Stradbroke, with the sun now down behind the farthest hills. As the hazy blue of evening was settling uniformly on this densely wooded country, the first stars started to pinpoint the sky.

Unsure in this light as to the particular ridge down which we should start our descent, we waited in the cool silence until the Southern Cross and its companions, the Pointers, came into view. Several dingoes called to one another not far from where we sat; no doubt fully aware of our presence. For those unused to this drawn-out, wolf-like call suddenly rending the still night, it can be disquieting. But in my experiences dingoes appear to be shy, private animals, preferring to melt into the forest when they detect human presence.

When the evening sky was a dark blue, we could clearly pick out our 'map in the sky'. My companion had not heard of this method of finding due south (the direction we needed to travel) by using connecting imaginary lines from both these groups of stars, and dropping a perpendicular line to determine south.

Once orientated, we commenced our return trip to Black Mountain station, experiencing in the dark sensations different from those of our ascent in daylight. As our eyes became less useful to us, our ears were our 'eyes of the night', and our minds concentrated on sounds we could well have missed had they been made in daylight. The flap of a bat's wing as it flew close to our faces, the snap of a distant twig, perhaps by a wombat or wallaby on its nocturnal feeding round; the swoosh of an owl flying almost imperceptibly overhead: all such sounds had greater clarity when one was concentrating in the darkness.

It was a slow trip back to base, but fortunately the kitchen stoves were still stoked, and Keith, anxious to hear of our findings, soon prepared plates of bacon and eggs, accompanied by numerous mugs of tea.

I saw Keith only once more before his death and regret that I never had an opportunity to share experiences in the bush either with him or with Norman Wakefield, whose natural history exploits are legend. Norman's interests and his knowledge of Gippsland were broad; fortunately he lectured widely and was able to pass on some of this in his books and papers before his untimely death.

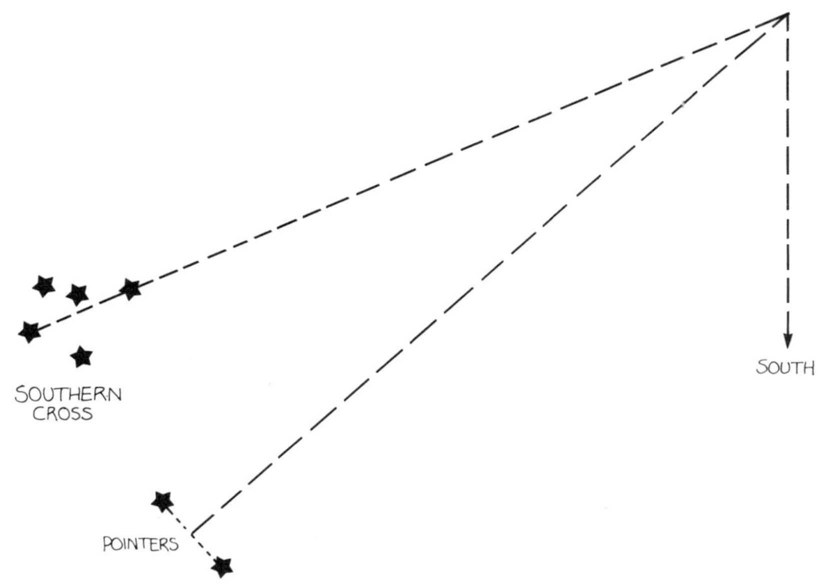

Finding south using a 'map in the sky'

4 CHINAMAN'S BEACH

WILSONS PROMONTORY VICTORIA

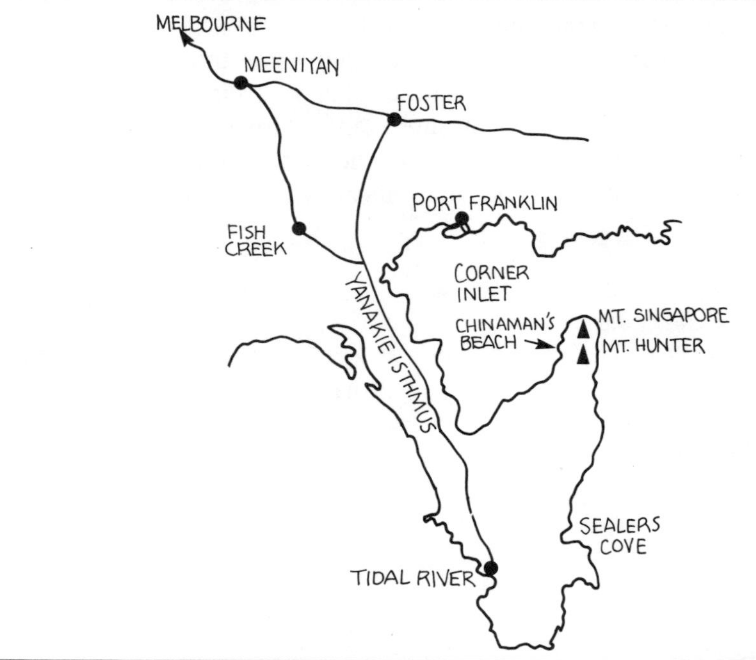

In the early 1970s I was asked by a botanist friend to investigate a record of *Grevillea alpina* at Wilsons Promontory. The indicated locality was on the slopes of Mt Hunter, on Singapore Peninsula, the most north-easterly tip of the Prom. Knowing that this was far from the normal distribution zones of *Grevillea alpina*, and knowing also that *G. lanigera* is not uncommon on these granite hills, I doubted the record. Still, this remote part of a beautiful area was one I had not visited, so I agreed to check it out.

I made arrangements with a fisherman at Port Franklin to ferry two friends and myself across to Chinaman's Beach. This was achieved at high tide on a calm, early spring morning, crossing sand bars on which fish could be easily detected, and channels so dark that we could only guess at what they held. We dropped anchor in shallow water off the white, narrow beach, and ferried our gear to a camp site under what was then known as *Casuarina stricta*, the drooping she-oak.

It has been determined that this long-standing name is now illegitimate, and this beautiful small tree, with fine pendulous branchlets, has the new name of *Allocasuarina verticillata*. The specific name *stricta* was misleading, since this dominant coastal plant is anything but rigid in habit.

A permanent stream cut through the low cliff behind our camp; and the water, though sweet, had the familiar light tea colour so often found in creeks which run through heathland. Since we had arranged for a pick-up at high tide early on the next afternoon, we wasted no time in investigating our surroundings. Within ten minutes, and in the first section of heathland, we found *Grevillea lanigera* growing as a low grey shrub. The leaves of this soft plant are small and blunt and their grey appearance is due to soft hairs which clothe them. A few of the shell-pink flowers were present, making a positive identification possible. It was not until I was checking my collection, some weeks later, against the specimens held at Melbourne University that I realised that both collections had been made from the same spot.

Now satisfied that we had cleared up this anomaly, we decided to investigate as much of the gradual granite slopes of Mt Hunter as our time would allow. Because of the exposed situation and the action of southerly winds, it was only in gullies that vegetation reached much above waist height. Much of this almost unbroken low swathe of vegetation was comprised of *Hakea* and *Acacia* species, many of which had rigid, sometimes needle-like leaves. The inevitable pricks and scratches we suffered walking through such an unyielding tangle ensured that our pace was slow, so that we observed items of interest we might easily have otherwise overlooked. Among these were some of the smaller ground orchids, which were found in various sites, but often in pockets of deeper sand where a break occurred in the dense canopy.

It was in one of these pockets that we found *Corybas unguiculatus,* the small helmet-orchid, so named because of the shape of the flower. Later we found species of sun orchid, one of which we could not identify at the time. We later found that it was *Thelymitra ixioides,* the dotted sun orchid.

Records show that approximately eighty species of orchids occur throughout the Prom. It is an impressive number, and though some are rare and not often seen this is a rewarding hunting ground for those with a particular interest in ground orchids.

Hakeas, four species of which occur here, all provide nectar and habitat for small birds, and doubtless for *Cercartetus nanus,* the pigmy possum, which frequents heathlands and banksia woodlands. The three hakeas which occur on or around the Mt Hunter heathland, *H. sericea, H. teretifolia* and *H. ulicina,* mostly have white perfumed flowers. Occasionally plants of *H. sericea* can be found with pink flowers, a colour variant more commonly found west of Melbourne. *H. ulicina,* which has flattened stiff leaves, also sports pink flowers in some populations.

The gradual climb to the flattish summit of Mt Hunter was completed as we walked through varying plant communities in which acacias were a strong element. Two of these, *A. oxycedrus* and *A. verticillata,* like the hakeas, let you know that you are walking through them, as their sharply pointed, rigid leaves are unyielding. This sclerophyll modification of leaves is one commonly found in the harsher dry landscapes of Australia. It contrasts sharply with the broader, softer leaves of plants constantly associated with shade and moisture, plants which grow not so very far away in deep gullies. Correa, epacris, dampiera, hibbertia, leptospermum; such a wealth of small attractive flowering plants shared this harsh mountain. From the top, the 360 degree view was magical, and open water could be seen at all points of the compass.

Having attained such a vantage point, we were reluctant to leave, but a sun low in the west indicated we should. We followed an alternate ridge down the north-west slope to enable us to examine some granite boulders which stood perhaps 4 metres above the heathland. Growing on the southern shaded side of one I found *Pyrrosia rupestris,* a small felted rock fern, which I had last seen at Genoa Peak in the far east of the state. It was so common on a few outcrops that I was surprised some months later, to discover that it was a new record for the Promontory. No doubt it occurs elsewhere in similar situations.

Unlike our walk up Mt Hunter, our downward journey was mostly spent looking down over Corner Inlet, and farther across the Yanakie Isthmus to Shallow Inlet.

Next day, as we sailed across the inlet and entered the mangrove-lined entrance to the Franklin River, we looked back at the peninsula which was now just an outline. The isolation of much of Wilsons Promontory ensures that such pristine areas can live and evolve with little interference or modification by man. To know that I or others may visit this area at a future time and find little changed underlines the value of conserving such a beautiful part of our heritage.

5 KOSCIUSKO

NEW SOUTH WALES

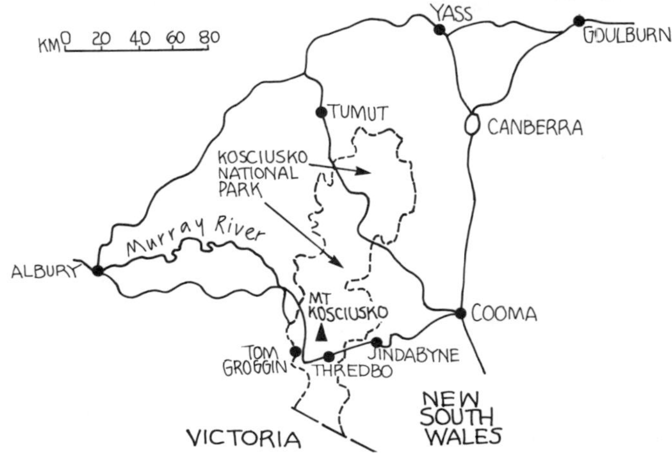

After a five day walking trip with Sue covering about 100 kilometres through Kosciusko National Park in New South Wales, the temptation to compare it with our own Victorian alpine areas was almost irresistible. But making comparisons would be like being unfaithful to an old friend, and therefore I will concentrate on describing those experiences of this area that were totally new to us.

The Kosciusko plateau is higher than its Victorian counterpart, has almost permanent snow patches, and was glaciated until recent geological times. These three factors produce a different topography to that south of the border (and only about 130 kilometres as the crow flies) and support the development of plants not found elsewhere in the high country. It is the numbers and extent of some species there, which are only scattered in areas such as the Bogong High Plains, that give breadth to the landscape.

One plant, *Podocarpus lawrencei*, the plum pine, occurred extensively on granite outcrops, or as colonies, on and over the large areas of glacial erratic rocks. Erratics are large areas of varying sized rocks that were randomly deposited as the glaciers retreated. *Podocarpus* is like many plants in cold climates; slow growing, it sprawls across the warmer rock surfaces to gain additional energy for growth. The rate of growth, as with most plants in areas where temperatures are high for only a short time, may be as little as a quarter of a millimetre a year in increment of the trunk. One specimen I measured had a trunk circumference of 11 centimetres, which would make it approximately 300 years old.

The action of old glaciers has now left a series of cirque lakes which are fed almost constantly from the permanent snow on the eastern flanks. These in turn overflow through tarns or directly to form the head-waters of the main small streams.

These meet quickly before elevation has greatly diminished to become what we know as the Snowy River.

For the walker or sightseer, the presence of so much water is refreshing and visually pleasing. Above the cool moisture of the lakes, which support a dense plant population, are communities situated on the windswept ridges which are stark in comparison. These are the Feldmarks, open, harsh, stony areas which support little plant life.

One plant invariably found on the leeside is a *Coprosma* species, the male flowers of which are tubular and yellow. On the female plants, whose flowers are inconspicuous, are squashy orange berries with an identical smell to those of *Coprosma repens,* the familiar 'mirror plant' of old gardens. This compact shrub is one of the 20 or more endemic plants found in the Kosciusko area.

One other, *Ranunculus anemoneus* – the largest flowering, most vigorous of our Australian buttercups – can be found in a range of sites, but is most outstanding when seen in association with receding snow patches. It occupies a similar niche to *Caltha introloba,* the marsh marigold, but is still in flower much later in summer. The large white-to-cream flowers with yellow centres can be 7 centimetres across, making them by far the largest flowering of the eight species of *Ranunculus* which occur at Kosciusko. It has not yet been widely grown in cultivation, but its appearance on drier rocky slopes indicates a hardiness that may be worth exploiting.

As we walked through the National Park, I was able to observe the restoration of areas previously damaged by cattle grazing. Some plants, grazed almost to the point of extinction, have gained a new life after more than 20 years. One of these, *Chionochloa frigida* (broad-leaved tussock grass), originally covered steep slopes, often above the tarns. Here, its bunching golden tussock habit contrasts with the darker green of many of the squatter plants that grow in this association. An old illustration I have seen shows perhaps 200 cattle grazing on *Carex gaudichaudiana*, a small sedge occupying the wet perimeters of lakes and tarns. This appealing plant, so important for water purity and as an erosion control, has recovered and now shows little sign of that former concentrated cropping.

The genus *Grevillea* has long held a fascination for me and *G. victoriae*, the only red-flowering plant in the alpine community, has its highest known distribution at Sentinel Peak, near Mt Kosciusko. This isolated point is reached by walking down and across a narrow rocky ridge, exhilarating in its sheerness either side of the narrow path. The *Grevillea* was much more prostrate than other populations I have seen. It is only 30-60 centimetres high, but has a considerable spread. This species, in many forms, has proved a useful garden shrub of three metres and is one of the parents of many of the well-known 'Poorinda' group of hybrids.

Many species of *Ranunculus* or buttercups grow here in a range of habitats. The smallest and daintiest, *R. millanii*, grows as a fine mat in muddy, moist depressions, and is often partly submerged. It also grows in moist, peaty soils associated with garden water areas, and will colonise a substantial area. Found on the margins of the wetter areas, *R. dissectifolius* is taller with bright yellow flowers on stalks 15 centimetres high. It, too, favours open, moist, but well-drained peaty soil, and will not outgrow its pot too quickly if grown as a container specimen.

One group found in both wet and dry sites was of those plants we commonly refer to as daisy flowers. Two yellow ones in particular caught my attention. *Microseris lanceolata*, the native dandelion, and also a close relative of the yam, has clumping felted leaves and large sunny flowers held face upward on stalks 30 centimetres tall. This habit made it stand out in the tussock grasslands throughout which it was abundant. Alpine groundsel is the common name for the other bright yellow daisy, *Senecio pectinatus*. This plant has crenate, lobed small leaves lying almost flat to the ground. These provide an interestingly textured carpet, above which the flowers are conspicuously held. The robust nature of both suggests they would acclimatise to a garden environment in which a cool, moist, well-drained root run was provided.

It is interesting to consider that even though the roof of Australia is a cold, harsh, snow-covered environment in winter, the intensity of the sun in the latter part of summer left me with a peeling nose and sunburnt back. But despite the heat the soils were moist; and correct soil preparation (apart from providing shade, semi-shade or full sun) is essential for the growing of these plants in a garden.

Craspedias, whose common name Billy Buttons is not universally recognised but aptly describes the shape of the flower heads, are a complex group of plants. Some are still known as *Craspedia species A B C D E* or *F* at this stage, rather than by a specific epithet. This in no way detracts from their charm with their combinations of white, yellow or orange flower heads, and their foliage of fine and argent grey or broad and soft green. They occupy a range of sites, often the dominant plant in the association.

As yet, we have only attempted a limited range of alpine plants in horticulture. Time and familiarity, with an understanding of growing conditions, will doubtless result in our seeing many more in gardens in the near future.

6 ALPINE FLOWERS

VICTORIA

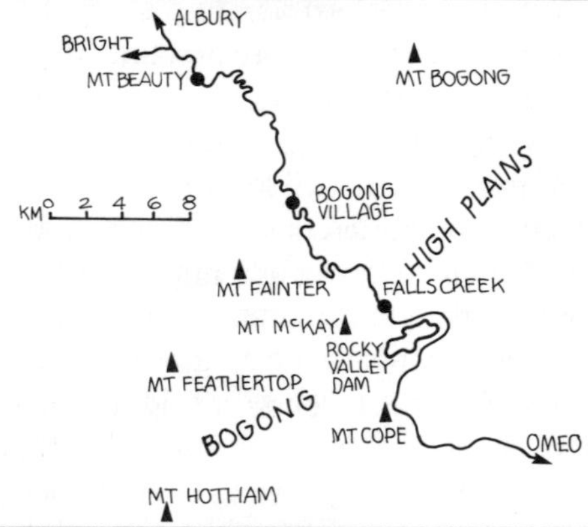

Occasionally I am tempted not to talk about areas of particular beauty or restfulness that are personal favourites. But the responsibility of sharing the pleasure and peace of our bushland soon overcomes any selfish motive. Victoria's high country, which occupies much of the north-east corner, is one area of great beauty at all times of the year. Surprisingly, relatively few people visit it and become involved in its simple beauty in summer or autumn. Flowering commences during these two seasons, even while the snow still covers much of the ground in early summer. Much of this flowering and later colourful shows are hardly appreciated by those people who simply drive through the high country, seldom leaving their cars as they glance at the broad views.

There is a sense of time standing still in the alpine area, no doubt induced by a return to simple activities and unhurried programmes. And it does take time to fully appreciate and become involved in the changing plant communities, much of them in typical alpine form standing no more than millimetres above the peaty soil.

My companions and I started a one-day walk, during a week-long visit, at a patch of wet ground below a sheet of melting snow. Within a hundred metres this imperceptibly moving water was joined from slopes on either side by half a dozen streams that came from secret sources. A small creek was formed, and within metres it could be heard running over pebbles and cutting down into the rich black peaty earth. Walking beside these streams as they meander through, over and under the combinations of sphagnum moss, *Baeckea gunniana*, *Epacris paludosa* and *Epacris glacialis* is to witness a world in miniature. The spring you feel in your feet comes from the layers of moss and other plants, perhaps 60 centimetres or more thick, on which you walk. Often these layers close over the clear, fast-running stream, or, they may be so dense and saturated that the stream runs over them, using them as its bed.

Suspended miniature billabongs are testimony to constant changing flow, and it is often in these that you find many of the *Ranunculus* species flowering either on the edge of or submerged beneath shallow water. These buttercup-like flowers, in shiny butter-coloured yellow or cream, and mostly with finely divided foliage, colonise many of the marsh edges and grasslands. *Ranunculus millanii*, one of the smallest flowering species, is the dominant plant of these areas. Used in similarly moist situations in landscaping, it will form compact mats by its layering habit.

A further pleasure in any familiar area is to find, for the first time, a plant in flower known to you previously only by its foliage. For many summers I had seen the small compact foliaged mounds of *Stackhousia pulvinaris* dotted between the snow grass, but never in flower. This year, though, the bright yellow-cream, five-petalled, star-like flowers covered these mounds. Even before we discovered our first groups of plants their perfume, a rich fruit-salad sweetness, reached us on a light breeze from 30 metres away.

For the rest of the day we delighted in the double pleasure of the perfume, followed by a new patch of flowering *Stackhousia*. This plant must surely give off one of our most heady perfumes from such small flowers. On this and following days the pleasure of discovery continued, and change of habitat or aspect brought new delights. The cream of *Phebalium squamulosum* contrasted with the bright yellow of *Phebalium phylicifolium*, both set among the purple of *Hovea purpurea* – the first two being shrubs to a metre high, the third often only 15 centimetres high. In association with these, the first yellow flowers were appearing on *Bossiaea foliosa* and on the alpine mint, *Prostanthera cuneata*. There is continual change, with the broad scene appearing dominated by specific plants whose place is then taken by others as soil or aspect changes.

Structurally, the dominant plant, which is also the only tree, is *Eucalyptus pauciflora*. On windswept hillsides, its gnarled and misshapen crown squats on top of a sturdy trunk. On the lee side, where the wind is less severe and the temperature not quite as low, the branches, though still chunky in structure, are more open and the crown taller. The smooth bark progresses through a range of seasonal colourings from olive-green to red, grey, and white. Around Fall's Creek village the sub-species *debeuzevillei*, incorrectly recorded only from Jounama to Kiandra in the Snowy Mountains region, is a dominant, much taller tree. It can be readily distinguished from traditional *E. pauciflora* by its larger buds, seed capsules, and fruits.

In this protected northern pocket, *Stylidium graminifolium*, the widespread trigger plant, colonises along with Poa or snow grass species, and *Parahebe* (formerly *Veronica*) *derwentiana*. The 'trigger plant', which can be found growing from the alpine snowfields to the edge of salt water on Wilsons Promontory, has large rosetted leaves and dark or light pink flowers densely clustered on upright stems which may reach to 60 centimetres or more. *Parahebe* has dentate leaves and is a shrub around 60-90 centimetres, with its pale mauve, butterfly-attracting flowers held above in eye-catching racemes.

Not far from this slope, I recently found for the first time the alpine form of *Eriostemon myoporoides*, the 'large-leaved wax flower'. Unlike other forms from moister but lower elevations such as at Toolangi (Vic.), this was a compact dense shrub less than a metre in height. The flowers were displayed in profusion, and the massed buds were rose pink in colour. We all considered it deserved the title native daphne because, though it lacked this plant's strong perfume, it was its equal in habit and flower. This *Eriostemon* has a long history of development. It is to be found not only in the high snow country, but also on ancient low sandstone hills in the NSW Riverina.

The only red-flowering alpine plant, *Grevillea victoriae*, which holds its buds in a dormant state during the snow season, is a strong component of these less elevated slopes. Named by Baron von Mueller to honour Queen Victoria, it, too, has a disjunct distribution, throughout alpine and highland areas of Victoria, NSW, and the ACT. It can be found as close to Melbourne as Mt Torbreck, where a small population occurs; and at Lake Mountain, farther to the north-east, it grows in profusion.

The currawong, with its clear plaintive call, is the bird most associated with the high country, and will always be found as a regular visitor to lodges or camp sites to take advantage of the extra food, especially when heavy snow is around. It is a large crow-sized bird, either pied or grey.

Only once have I encountered a large snake above the snowline. It was a black snake, but did not have the lustrous colouring of its lowland counterpart; it was a dull grey/black, with underparts of bronze rather than red. It was curled up on a pile of broken granite along the aqueduct, and was evidently just coming out of winter hibernation.

It is not the reptiles or even the animals that enchant you in the high country but the wonderful profusion of plants, streams, sphagnum bogs, and the clean, clear air. Following recent further National Park proclamations for alpine areas in Victoria, there have been strong objections from cattle association representatives. One can understand, if not accept, these objections and the emotion behind them. Grazing the high country has been traditional for a number of families for many generations; it is the sort of stuff on which legends such as 'The Man from Snowy River' were based.

I have walked many times across the high country, and slept or sought shelter in the slab and tin huts erected by and for the cattlemen who use them during mustering at the end of each summer season. There is no doubt that there is a strong feeling of romance about it all; but time and new understanding make changes inevitable.

All that could be said for and against the parks has been said time and again, and the decisions have been made. We all have had to adjust to dramatic change in our lives. Social and moral mores are constantly in flux; technology is developing at an alarming pace; and those of us conducting businesses have had to be innovative and more productive to survive the extreme cost pressures of the last decade. Agriculture, too, has had to introduce more efficient cropping and husbandry techniques that would not have been dreamt of twenty years ago.

Just as a multitude of manufacturers had to cease polluting rivers with factory wastes and invest large sums of money installing treatment works, so, too, will the comparatively few cattlemen affected have to invest in new and more efficient ways of producing their product. They will have to recognise that farming is a business, as well as a family way of life, and that the use of land is a temporary privilege; in fact, a stewardship. The cattlemen have faced great challenges before, and have had the strength and will to overcome them. No doubt they will show the same resilience in the future and adjust to the new demands in their industry.

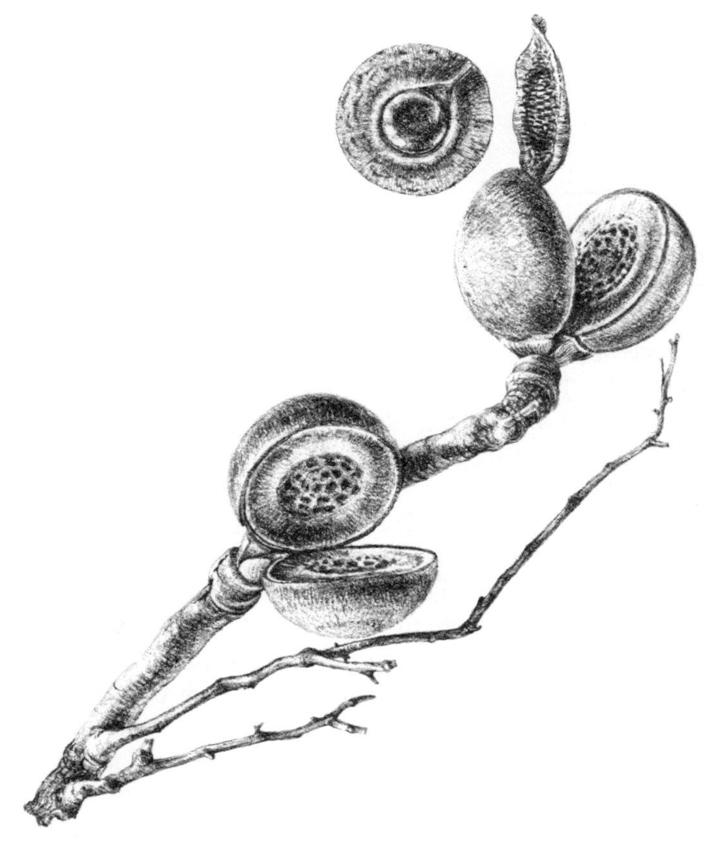

Hakea platysperma

7 GRANITE OUTCROPS

& MOUNTAINS OF NORTH-EAST VICTORIA

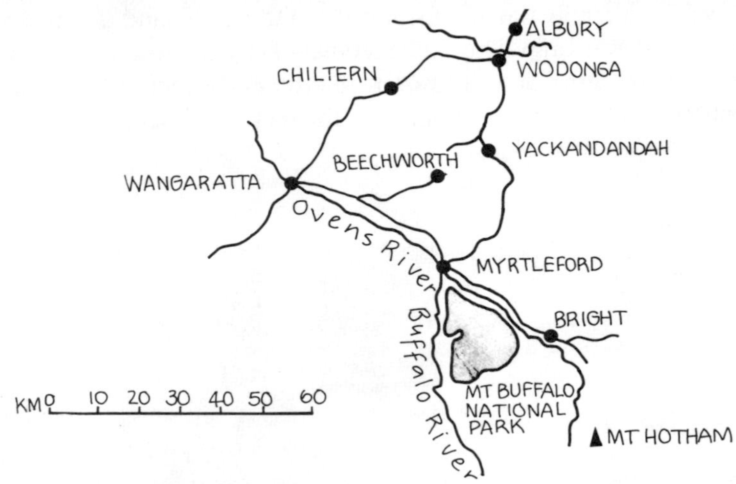

From the middle of July, colour starts to show on the grey-green palette that breaks the surface of granite outcrops in north-eastern Victoria. The dominant hue of tree and shrub has as its backdrop the lichen-covered speckled grey of the granite itself. These ancient massifs, which often support plants no longer extant on surrounding country, began the move towards their present status as molten masses far below the earth's crust. As these masses welled up, often displacing the country-rock above upwards by thousands of metres, they began their cooling processes. Insulated by the rock above, cooling was often so slow that crystallisation, the structure which differentiates the grainy-ness of granite from the fine texture of basalt, was able to take place gradually. What we now see, standing clear of the surrounding landscape, are the exposed weathered remains of much greater mountains or massifs. The process still continues before our gaze, but at a rate we can hardly discern, even though it is measurable in our lifetime.

Plants have both survived through and adapted to the dramatic changes; new species have appeared, and colonisation upwards by species from lower ground has occurred. Many have found suitable niches, where they appear to be the dominant plant: soil depth and available moisture encouraging their growth during good times, and remaining sufficient to ensure their survival during adverse seasons.

At Flat Rock, west of Beechworth, *Micromyrtus ciliata*, a small member of the broad and diverse Myrtaceae family, is a beautiful example of such survival.

It occupies, in a massed effect and often no more than 45 centimetres high, pockets where soil formed by the decomposing granite and plant matter has attained sufficient depth to support growth. I have seen these colonies, during extended hot, rainless periods, look as though they were dying. The fine foliage is often orange or yellow and seems quite desiccated. The plants remain this way for months, until the onset of rain and cooler weather bring about a dramatic change.

The appearance now changes from death-like to the green of life. New growth shoots from dormant stems, and flower buds begin to sprout. By early August the flat tops of the plant colonies range in colour from white through pale pink to dark pink and red, just prior to the full burst of flower. This changes quite dramatically back to white and light pink as the opened flowers become the dominant display.

While all this has been taking place, *Acacia buxifolia* changes from a small grey shrub, playing its part in the overall vegetation community, to a golden prima donna, leaping out from the chorus line. Soon a further colour, that of royal purple, enters the picture. Sometimes cascading over the ground, or perhaps climbing lightly into the branches of small shrubs and trees, *Hardenbergia violacea* vies with the gold of *Acacia* for attention; and this combination would enhance any garden.

The observant naturalist will detect, as he moves from one granite outcrop to the next, new individual plants, as well as communities that have adapted to or evolved to meet the specific site advantages or limitations. On some, such as in the Warby Ranges near Wangaratta, two plants in particular survive as indicators of obviously greater populations which once grew here and on the surrounding plains. The first, *Acacia triptera,* has its main area of distribution around Gurrulmundi in south central Queensland, a hotter, drier environment than the Warby Ranges. In Victoria, it occurs nowhere except on parts of the Warbys. The second, *Santalum lanceolatum,* is widespread throughout the drier interior of the continent, but occurs only as a single tree on the eastern face of this range, and at Boundary Bend on the Murray River.

I have encountered this phenomenon often, and not specifically on granite, where survivors hang on in the face of dramatic climate change. Such surviving plants contribute to our understanding of the jigsaw puzzle that time has designed. The fossil records show us how dramatic the changes have been, from an age in which the continent had much wetter weather and evolved a flora and fauna to suit this, to the present time when the drying-out process is still occurring.

Plants show remarkable inventiveness, with a new population evolving to fill the niche of those that find the going too tough. This ability of plants almost to hibernate in times of stress can be observed throughout the continent, and not only on granite massifs. Many, such as *Grevillea,* which had its origins in rainforest where it still happily thrives, can be seen adapting to the rigours of a desert summer.

The best known of Victoria's granite massifs is Mt Buffalo, situated near Myrtleford in the north-east of the state. Its present elevation of 1721 metres is low, compared to an estimated original height of nearly 5000 metres before the inexorable wearing down by rain, wind, frost and sun, of such a leviathan resulted in the generally low profile we know today. Relatively isolated from other high country, Mt Buffalo stands out in the generally low surrounding countryside, its steep-sided flanks presenting an imposing sight. Mt Buffalo is the last bastion of the Great Dividing Range, and to the west and north-west the profile of the land is relieved only occasionally by outliers of any appreciable elevation.

While Mt Buffalo supports many plants which are also to be found at similar altitudes in alpine and subalpine areas nearby, three endemic species have developed during long periods of isolation from outside influences. *Eucalyptus mitchelliana* is a small, clean-trunked tree with fine foliage which can be found scattered throughout woodlands near the present chalet. *Acacia dallachiana*, with large, thick leaves and rod-shaped, catkin-like flowers, is found in dense populations at lower elevations; while the third species, *Baeckea crenatifolia*, a shrub with small aromatic foliage and white flowers, frequents the banks of creeks.

More than four hundred plants have been recorded for the park, a number which makes this an important island for many species which have their most north-westerly distribution here.

I know of nowhere else in Victoria that one can find the following five species of *Grevillea* growing and exhibiting the selection and utilisation of habitat. As the road from Porepunkah in the north winds up and around the lower contours, one may glimpse a small, grey-leaved plant, possibly with waxy pink and white flowers, growing out of the gravelly soil of the road cutting. If one stops and inspects the cutting and the vegetation above on foot, one finds clumps of this small *Grevillea lanigera* (*lanigera* means woolly) growing among the grasses which accompany it. Further investigation reveals that many of the clumps are joined underground by roots, and that what you are looking at are root suckers. Unlike other and often larger forms of this variable species, this one does not seem to set a great deal of seed and has instead chosen to perpetuate itself by suckering; it is a regional development and is only to be found on close handy hillsides.

Further on, before Eurobin Creek, a fine-foliaged, more upright small shrub can be seen in similar habitats. This is *Grevillea parvifolia*, whose many forms are popular in cultivation. While the small group of white or pink and white flowers are not large, they are perfectly in scale whereas more flamboyant flowers could look incongruous against its fine silvery habit. It is these attributes which have made this plant popular for using beside water areas in association with similar plants, or in areas limited in size where a bulky habit would be out of place.

The third of our collection, *Grevillea alpina*, can be seen to best effect beside the track to Eurobin Falls. Also a variable species, it is never (contrary to what its name implies) found in alpine areas. It is a plant of elevated forests and woodlands, extending to the Grampians in western Victoria, where it varies from a trailing small shrub with waxy red and gold flowers, to an erect shrub of more than a metre. At Eurobin Falls it attains a similar height but has a small spreading canopy, umbrella-like in shape. The small hairy leaves turn back on the stems, and the red and yellow flowers are in small clusters on side shoots. Like all forms of *Grevillea alpina*, this one needs a gritty or stony well-drained soil if it is to grow satisfactorily in gardens. When it thrives, the colourful, nectar-laden flowers not only prove to be a source of visual pleasure but act as a magnet to nectar-feeding birds.

The final two grevilleas grow at the highest elevations, where they are covered in a mantle of snow for some months. The smaller of these, *Grevillea australis*, is not dissimilar to some forms of *G. parvifolia*, but with one major difference. The nectar exuded by its small flowers gives off a very strong perfume which is even more noticeable on warm summer evenings. It can often be found sprawling over granite boulders, sharing this space with such plants as *Podocarpus lawrencei*, a small alpine pine, or *Oxylobium alpestre*, which has orange-yellow pea flowers.

A reason suggested for plants adopting these postures is that they can absorb growth-promoting warmth from the rock, thereby extending what can be a short growing season after the heavy snow has thawed.

In an environment in which many plants have small foliage and white, purple or orange flowers, the large grey-green leaves and red russet flowers of *Grevillea victoriae* make it a singularly noticeable plant. The pendulous buds of this common large shrub develop in late summer and autumn and are held in a dormant state while covered in snow. The combination of higher temperature, when the snow melts, and greater light intensity initiates flowering and fertilisation, and seed setting occurs well before the next snow falls.

Mt Buffalo is deservedly one of our popular Victorian tourist attractions, catering for a wide spectrum of passive or active recreation. It is challenging for the walker or climber, interesting for the natural historian, and a beautiful environment for those visitors who are merely seeking scenic stimulation. Good winters provide wide scope for cross country and limited down-hill skiing, but very good snow cover seems now to be the exception rather than the rule.

8 MT CAROLINE

WESTERN AUSTRALIA

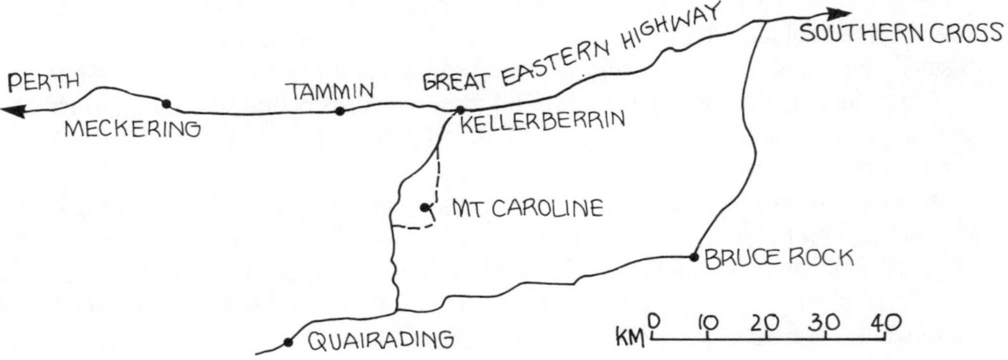

The recorded habitat for *Eucalyptus caesia* is a series of low profile granite outcrops in Western Australia. These are situated mainly in the area north-west of Southern Cross, but some outliers occur west of here and to the south of the main highway to Perth. It was to one of these, Mt Caroline, south of Kellerberrin, that we headed for a break after crossing the Nullarbor during a trip west.

There is no feeling of isolation about these more southern outcrops, since most are surrounded by rural activity. Wheat fields and grazing sheep infringe almost to the base of the vast rock slopes, and farmhouses are visible from most high points.

Many of the populations of *E. caesia* are on northerly rocks that are more remote and generally of a grander scale. Once through into the lightly timbered and grassed amphitheatre formed by the separate peaks of Mt Caroline, one quickly forgets the openness of the surrounding country.

The dominant small tree, *Acacia acuminata* (known as 'jam' because of the smell of the cut timber) is a favourite nesting habitat for small fly-catching birds. It occurs on the deeper soil of the flat areas, but once the profiles become shallower it gives way to plants that can tolerate less soil depth. It is in these pockets below large boulders that *Eucalyptus caesia* is found; and even though a large number occur here none reach the stature of northern populations. All of this graceful, small tree's familiar and beautiful aspects, which have endeared it to gardeners throughout temperate Australia and overseas, were still present though: pendulous habit, white waxy bloom on branches and buds, the large pink groups of flowers, and the peeling red-brown bark.

Most references to this plant still include the use of the Aboriginal word *Gungurru*, now known to be more correctly applied to *Eucalyptus woodwardii*. This tall, weeping tree differs markedly from *E. caesia*, having very grey foliage and bright yellow flowers in winter and spring. *Eucalyptus woodwardii* is known only from small populations growing in the Victoria Desert area of Western Australia, a hundred kilometres or so east of Kalgoorlie. Like *E. caesia* it has adapted to cultivation, in this instance where rainfall is low and drainage good.

While *Eucalyptus caesia* grows within the relatively limited protection of large granite outcrops it is fortunate that these rock massifs will remain inviolate, and that this unique tree will have a safe repository in which to grow and reproduce its kind. Here, too, is possibly the most southerly distribution point for *Grevillea petrophiloides*, a plant more commonly found farther north in drier areas.

It is tempting for an author to claim that the plants and places he is writing about are the most spectacular, beautiful, or remote. Yet no one could dispute the unusual beauty, habit, and style of *Grevillea petrophiloides*. It is a large though visually fine shrub whose bright pink brushes of flowers, which start as an inky blue, are held well out from and above the deeply lobed narrow leaves by long leafless stems. There they parade themselves in their hundreds, demanding attention from pollination agents, competing for the favours of the small honeyeating birds which inhabit their region. The nectar itself is sweet and copious: a cup formed by the palm of your hand is soon filled by the shaking of a few blooms. The cooler, moister conditions here, just south of Kellerberrin, produced in this unusual *Grevillea* a stature far exceeding that of the plants we saw around Wongan Hills and farther northward.

While no other individual plants attained either the beauty or the dominance of *G. petrophiloides* at this secluded haven, many others were securely filling niches, providing nesting and feeding habitat for bird, insect, or animal in return for pollen distribution. It is a marvellous web of life into which the mobile and the anchored are inextricably interwoven.

All life on these granite monoliths has to adapt to extreme climatic change, season after season; and it is only those life forms which we now see doing this so successfully that have survived millions of years of selection and rejection. This resilient selection can cope with an environment which varies from very wet and frost-prone in winter, to extremely hot and dry during summer.

One plant, a small lily, *Borya nitida*, has such a dried orange-brown appearance in summer that it appears dead. The small mounds colonise pockets of shallow soil and seem at best to have a tenuous hold on life. *Borya*, though, has adapted tenaciously to its chosen niche, and its summer appearance indicates a stage of dormancy from which it quickly awakens with the first rain. Quickly the small sharp leaves turn green, and the delicate heads of white flowers come into bud and then open. I have grown *Borya* either in a rock pocket or in a container for more than a decade, and apart from the first summer, when by their colour they exhibited a dormant state, they have maintained a green appearance. Other plants while not exhibiting the same dramatic colour change to their foliage, obviously 'wind down' their internal systems so that they can cope with the extremes of summer. In the northern hemisphere, the flora becomes dormant in response to snow and very low temperatures; conversely, in Australia, the temperate zone flora responds in a like fashion to high temperatures.

A few days later we drove west from Mt Caroline through the sad, weed-choked narrow road verges of extant flora struggling for survival and bravely flowering. These remnants of the once beautiful plains can have but a short time left in existence: weeds, sprays, burning, and diminution of gene diversity, will all eventually take their toll. It is a sad story repeated constantly throughout this southern region of Western Australia, one of the most important floristic areas in the world.

The freedom of all to exercise their right to enjoy nature and space is constantly being eroded. I know that there would be a void in my life, in my spirit, if the restorative value of an uncluttered, minimally affected wilderness were denied to me. Retaining our right to this heritage carries the responsibility of fighting for its retention and preservation.

While headlands of the New South Wales coast can be windswept, inlets make idyllic camp sites. The margins of these zones support populations of often-maligned mangroves, like the striking specimen above. Right, long flowering stalks of *Grevillea petrophiloides* rise out of the finely divided grey leaves. This southern granite-dwelling population, of a usually sand-plain species, partly screens the open farmland which surrounds its Mt Caroline habitat

The beautiful orchid at left, *Caladenia flava,* can be found either in pockets of soil on top of Mt Caroline and similar granite massifs, or among the mallee heath around their bases. Also at Mt Caroline *Boyra nitida,* below, looks dessicated but is alive and flowering. Opposite, Sue and Bill by a pool on the Bogong High Plains; this links with others to become the Kiewa River. Even in summer, wet-weather gear may be needed to ward off sudden cold changes. *Hovea longifolia* var. *montana,* below right, shows how alpine plants extract any available warmth, by hugging a granite rock. It often grows in large communities, as a shrub to about 80 centimetres

In protected gullies, below the windswept mountain tops, the widespread rosette-leaved pink *Stylidium graminifolium* (above left) often grows en masse with the equally profuse *Parahebe derwentiana.* At right, *Acacia triptera,* readily recognised by its spurred foliage, ranges from south central Queensland to the Warby Ranges in Victoria. The red laterite soils found over vast areas of south-western Australia support numerous combinations of colourful plants. Below, blue *Dampiera* and *Glischrocaryon*

9 PEAK CHARLES

WESTERN AUSTRALIA

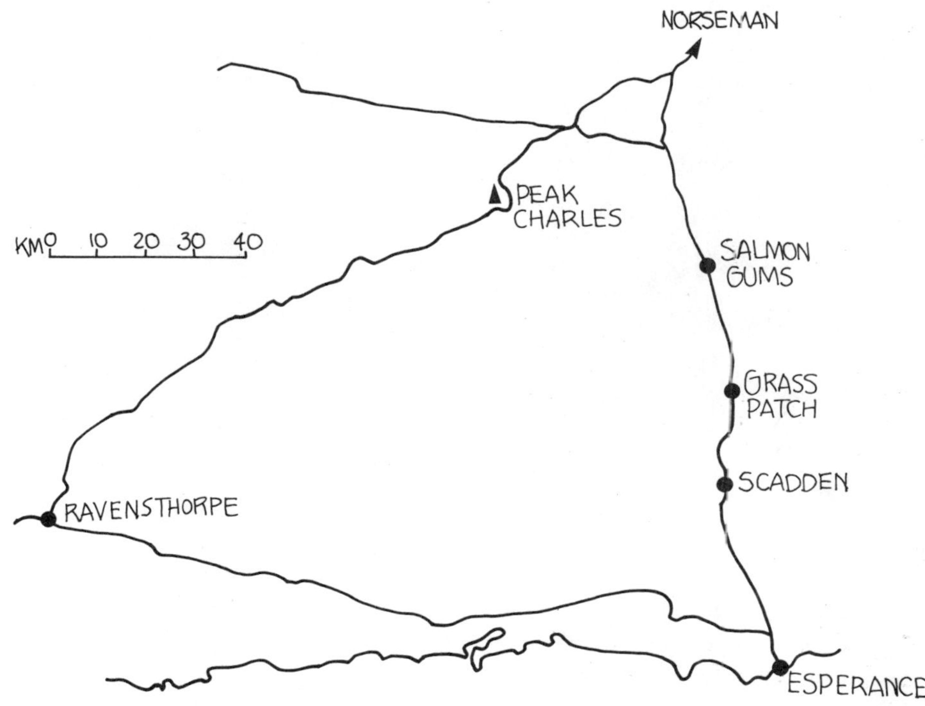

Rising out of the low mallee heathland some 100 kilometres north-west of Esperance on the southern Western Australian coast, the domes of Peak Charles and Peak Eleanora dominate the flat, broad topography. Just by standing on the roof of your vehicle in this country you gain sufficient height to gaze across hundreds of square kilometres to the four points of the compass.

While granite underlies much of Western Australia, it is not often seen above the ground. Cape le Grand to the south-east, the high ground around both Esperance to the south and Albany to the south-west, provide relief; but vast areas of mallee and heathland stretch almost uninterrupted between. The great age of these exposed granite mountains and outcrops, in some instances around 2000 million years, or half the current known age of the planet, explains not only the rounded, often low, weathered profile they exhibit, but also why many often carry on their ancient flanks such singularly individual flora.

These massifs have been islands on numerous occasions, with seas lapping at their flanks for vast periods of time, even as recently as the quaternary period. Those plants that did colonise rocks during long periods when the sea retreated were genetically cut off when once again the seas invaded. Subtle local pressure for survival brought about eventual change, and opportunistic species took hold and flourished against less resilient ones.

The well-known *Eucalyptus caesia,* which forms colonies only on granite outcrops, does not extend this far south or east; an area north of Hyden, some 200 kilometres to the west, is its last southerly outlier. On Peak Charles, however, there grows a particular plant, *Calothamnus tuberosus,* which, as its specific name implies, exhibits a rare characteristic. In Western Australia it is currently regarded as the only member of the extensive Myrtaceae family (which includes eucalypts, melaleucas, and callistemons) which is known to possess a tuberous root system. This plant, with rigid needle-like leaves, can be found on exposed sites, its shallow root system firmly anchored beneath the exfoliating sheet rock.

These sheets are an interesting phenomenon in themselves, and often form shelters for small lizards and tiny dragons. The shelters, looking like Stonehenge bivouac tents, form when a smallish sheet of stone fractures down its length. By some means (perhaps the expansion and contraction due to extremes of temperature) the outside edges of both sections apply pressure inwardly, forcing the two inside edges up against each other. If the angle and line of fracture are compatible the centre gradually lifts.

I have observed small 'suburbs' of these tents on suitable rock types, many around 30-45 centimetres square, some much larger. Without disturbing these shelters, you can lie on your stomach and, by sighting along the space beneath, you will more often than not see a lizard or small snake sheltering from the extremes of weather.

A second *Calothamnus*, or 'net bush' as it is locally known, grows over extensive areas of Peak Charles. This species has less rigid, slightly hairy needle foliage and the typical bright red masses of claw flowers throughout spring.

These granite outcrops are alive with nectar-feeding birds and a number of plants provide for their main diet over many months. At the base of Peak Charles, I recall a steep-sided pocket in which a considerable depth of gritty soil had accumulated. Growing in this was a thicket of small trees, with the dwarf form of *Eucalyptus occidentalis*, growing to about 5 metres, being the dominant mallee. It was only July, but already the bright yellow flowers were spreading their nectar-laden perfume throughout this confined grove; and numerous birds were taking up residence.

Its raucous call, its size, and the fleshy red wattle of the 'red wattlebird' make this distinctive bird the most obvious member of this community. No doubt, even though these birds often build their nests much higher, they would make use of the low, dense melaleuca or acacia habitats that encircle the base of the peak. Of the other birds present, the white-plumed honeyeater was the most numerous, and small silvereyes were taking advantage of the numbers of insects feeding on the blossom. The importance of the surrounding mallee as nesting habitat for these seasonal visitors is readily apparent.

There was a strong sweet fragrance whose source took some detecting. It seemed to be close to our toilet site, a discreet area of sand tucked behind a patch of dense mallee comprising mainly *Acacia acuminata* and *Melaleuca hamulosa*. Returning from spending a few contemplative minutes in this private area, we all at some time remarked about the strong but delicate perfume coming from the mallee. All initially had looked towards the upper or middle canopy, seeking the source of the perfume: until, on one occasion, when inspecting a patch of *Diuris longifolia* on hands and knees, I came across this plant scarcely 15 centimetres above ground level. It was *Lomandra effusa*, a contrast to the *Diuris* (a 'donkey orchid' with beautiful brown and yellow colourings) with its short fine needle leaves and clusters of tiny flowers. There was no doubt, as the sweet perfume pervaded the area, that I had detected our bush toilet deodorant.

It is a further indication of the age of this and companion species when you realise that this tiny plant is found in all mainland states. Even though I had previously and subsequently observed this small lily in both Victoria and New South Wales, I did not recall its perfume being as strong as in this Western Australian population.

The knowledge that much of this country is under threat of total clearing for wheat farming is of great concern; already extensive corridors of it have been cleared for short-term agriculture. And short-term it will be, because the great quantity of salt lying just below the surface of most of this country rises quickly once the tree cover is removed and the land will be useless for cultivation. The floral diversity that has taken millions of years in isolation to evolve is replaced for a few brief years of return by a monoculture crop. The still popular 'pioneering the West' attitude needs to be tempered with an understanding of the irreversibility of these actions.

In the future, people in positions of decision-making may be judged not by the returns from wheat exported to Russia or a third world country but by their irresponsibility in allowing the elimination of a scientific storehouse that is still little understood. In the eighteen years that I have been visiting these areas, I have witnessed acts that can only be described as vandalism. The eradication of much of the southern populations of *Banksia occidentalis*, east of Esperance, is one illustration.

This species, which grows only in seasonal swamps, is limited to a few areas where ideal conditions exist. Many of these localities are only a few acres in extent, and as such constitute only a small percentage of areas considered for clearing. Was this factor, the rarity of the plant, and the unsuitability of its habitat for cropping, considered before clearing? Certainly it would appear not, and the now bare paddocks bear witness to the short-sightedness of those who cleared them.

10 GENOA RIVER

VICTORIA

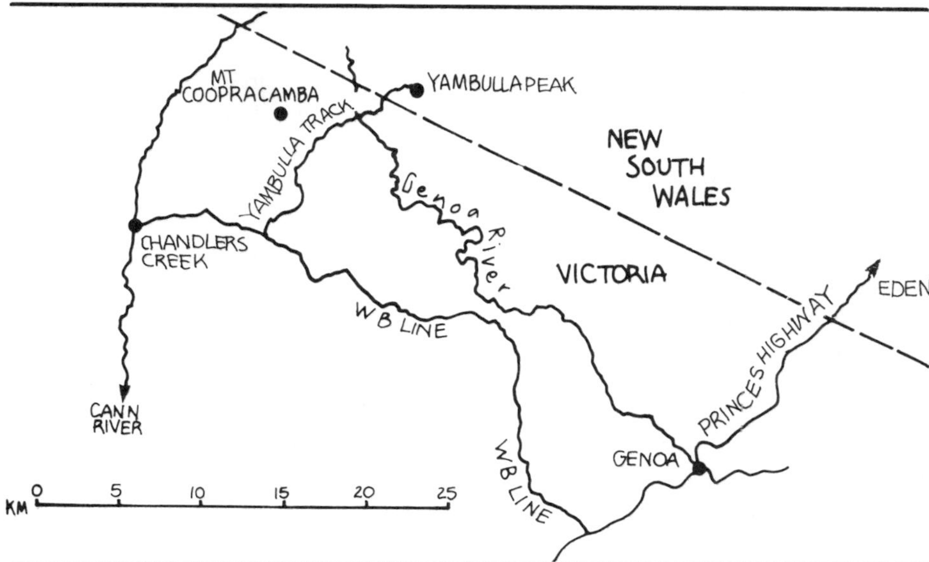

Many people believe they must travel great distances to see something new, and perhaps it is natural to feel that distant pastures are greener than what may be at their own doorstep. Certainly, if given the choice, I would visit the wildflower areas of southern Western Australia time and time again. But when my spirit is drawn to mountains, rivers, gorges and solitude, then my home state, Victoria, has most that I seek in its area of Gippsland.

The best-known river, one of only three that bisect the state from north to south, is the one to which so much romance is attached – the Snowy. With its small beginnings in New South Wales, beneath Mt Kosciusko, it becomes the beautiful river of pebbled beds and steep gorges in the middle stretches, and the broad waterway of the lower open farmland. It is not this better known river, though, with which this journey is involved; it is one farther west, the Genoa River, the last of the major waterways before the New South Wales border is reached.

Mallacoota Inlet is where the Genoa empties into the sea, through the Top Lake and Bottom Lake; and there is a part of the lower river which is well known as a popular holiday spot. The upper reaches, below the point where it crosses the Bonang Highway, are less well known, and certainly less accessible. I had visited the lower middle reaches previously by way of an easy side track at the eastern end of the WB Line, an access track that runs parallel to the Princes Highway but 30 kilometres to the north. The take-off point for the upper Genoa, though, is much farther west, and can be tackled only with a reliable four-wheel-drive vehicle. It is a track known as Yambulla Peak track, and it is 8.5 kilometres along the WB Line from the Cann Valley Highway turn-off.

I don't advocate the use of such vehicles unless it is necessary, but on this track it certainly is. There is an early drop into a narrow creek, with a very steep rise straight out and up. Traction can be difficult after rain. The balance of the journey until the final drop down to the river is easy, but this last stage is very steep, with broad outcrops of rock to negotiate. As we found at the end of our stay, these outcrops need to be handled slowly and with care in the steep climb out.

At this point of the river we found ourselves only a few kilometres below the border, and its course lay deep in gorges cut through ancient uplifted sandstone rock. The forest clothes the slopes right down to the bare rocks which indicate the high water mark. Here, the dominant tree is *Eucalyptus elata*, a peppermint with a tall straight trunk, clean save for a tight stocking of bark in the lower quarter. This graceful, large tree has a fine foliaged canopy, and while it is more abundant in similar habitats in New South Wales, it is also common along these east Gippsland rivers. Few plants have suffered the same confusion of identity as this tree, which has had four separate epithets applied to it; it has also been included under *E. radiata*. The latter, also a peppermint, differs chiefly in having tight, rough bark covering its trunk and branches. We encountered dense stands of it on higher, better drained ground, intermixed with the widespread *E. macrorhyncha*, one of the stringy-barks and often with *E. sieberi*, an ash with dark furrowed bark covering the trunk. Old trees of this species can be confused from a distance with *E. sideroxylon*, whose darker, harder bark appears in a series of longitudinal ridges and deep furrows.

All the previous species have white flowers, but this population of *E. sideroxylon* has large pink flowers, mostly in threes. It occurs in a thin belt across this part of Victoria, and these specimens, at a height of around 25 metres, were the biggest I ever recalled seeing.

The less steep slopes and the plateaus contained many plants we had not previously encountered in Victoria. The late Norman Wakefield, a well-known modern naturalist, had visited this area on a number of occasions, and had remarked on the unusual number of *Pomaderris* species. Though this great man of natural science was perhaps better known for his work with mammals, his contribution to botany was also extensive. From early childhood he ventured into remote areas, often in Gippsland, and his keen observations led him to discover many new treasures. We found many plants he had mentioned previously, and were pleased to come across some which he hadn't.

Pomaderris is a member of the world-wide family Rhamnaceae, which in Australia also includes species of the horticulturally desirable *Spyridium* and *Cryptandra* genera. Paradoxically, even though many *Pomaderris* species have larger and brighter flower heads, they have not gained the same horticultural acceptance. The smallest and possibly the most attractive species was *Pomaderris andromedifolia*, a shrub growing to little more than a metre high, with delightful – and unusual for Australia – bicoloured leaves. These oval leaves are about one centimetre long and silvery green in colour (or, in the case of aging leaves, brilliant orange or red). Although it was not the flowering season, this shrub's light, open appearance attracted us to collect propagation material. We were fortunate in obtaining a few plants from this stock; later when they did bloom, the plant was covered in small heads of golden flowers.

Just upstream from this group of plants are two further ones which occur in Victoria only at this point. One, *Allocasuarina nana* (formerly *Casuarina nana*), one of the smallest of the she-oaks, occupied a large platform covered in shallow soil derived from the sandstone. Few members of this dense population reached more than a metre in height. Like many such plants which grow in tough environments, when *Allocasuarina nana* is brought into cultivation, it grows to almost twice this height.

The second plant, *Patersonia longifolia*, would have been easily missed if we had not noticed the occasional blue, three-petalled, iris-like flower sitting down among the plant's fine grey leaves and the clumps of grasses which lightly covered the ground. One sometimes wonders about the appropriateness of some plant epithets: this plant, possibly the smallest-leaved in the genus (with leaves only fifteen centimetres long and about two millimetres wide), has been given the specific name *longifolia*. Fortunately we were able to find a few seeds still sitting in the bottom of the papery seed heads; and from these we subsequently grew and flowered some in our garden.

Two other *Patersonia* species were collected in this area, and while neither *P. sericea* nor *P. glabrata* are confined to this locality, outside New South Wales they are only found in eastern Victoria.

Along and above the river were a number of callistemons. *Callistemon subulatus*, which is mainly found in NSW, but extends westward in Victoria to Nowa Nowa, is one of the smaller bottlebrushes. The flowers of these are mostly red, but here they were a lustrous mauve. This fine-foliaged plant grows often in the most precarious positions. Its bent trunk shows the force of water that must innundate it for weeks on end during winter, but, held firmly by a tenacious root hold in rock crevices, it survives, flowers, and reproduces.

On higher rocky banks above the waterline, near an area of rolling and dipping rock strata, we found a smaller, paler flowered form of *Callistemon pallidus*. This is a form typical of eastern Gippsland, and not like the heavy-foliaged, deeper lemon-brushed form found on higher mountains north-east of Melbourne and at Wilsons Promontory.

As well, we found a *Callistemon* which we did not recognise. It was very erect in habit, attained 3 metres in height, and had a compact shape with a spread of less than half its height. It was not in flower, and as far as we could see it was confined to sandy shelves well above the normal water level. I did manage to find some seed, and the plants I grew have now flowered, bearing brushes

Genoa River and fossil detail (right)

of deep burgundy touched with mauve overtones. It does not appear to fit into any of the traditionally recognised species, and it would seem that further investigation is required.

It was while resting on the opposite bank that we found a deposit of small fossils – bedded in the sandstone strata. We had read of their existence, and their usefulness in determining the age of the rock on this river. There were any number of these small, often finger-sized fossils. Then, back on the Victorian side of the border, below where Yambulla Creek, flowing from the east, joins the Genoa River, we found a much larger fossil.

On this day we had been attempting to locate the area where some years previously a major discovery had been made by Norman Wakefield of ancient footprints, embedded on a shelf above the normal waterline. A reconstruction from these footprints suggested an animal around a metre in length, including a tail. It was an important discovery, because its recognised age related to the previously oldest known fossils from the Northern Hemisphere. We were sitting on a large pile of rock, a pile that had been deposited from higher up on the tall sandstone bluff behind us, when we spied an unusual marking on a square section of rock.

It was a block about 30 centimetres square, dark in colour and fine in texture; and it was not hard to imagine its having once been fine silt in a less turbulent part of a river or lake. On one surface was an impression of a section of a large leaf-like structure, not unlike that of *Asplenium*, the 'birds' nest' fern. We were to find later that this was a superficial resemblance only; and although specific identification has not been made it was suggested that the fossil closely resembled a *Lepidodendron*, an ancient plant known to have occurred in the area.

I walked back to camp, alternately cradling this block in my arms or balancing it on one or other shoulder. I used the excuse of a dingo calling near at hand to pause and ease my tired muscles. We were high above the river, looking down and across it to a broad sandy beach, wondering if the dingo would come into the open. It was only through a slight movement that we detected a wallaby crouched by the river's edge.

We were amazed that it stayed there with such danger close at hand. Through our binoculars, we discovered that it was very old, and possibly partly blind and deaf. We attempted to frighten it away to safety by throwing stones across the river, but it would not move, even when we shouted. As we left, to continue our return trip, the sun was dropping behind Mt Coopracamba, and silently we thought of the final drama that would be played out with the setting sun. Perhaps nature knew best.

It was clear from the debris caught against tree trunks and deposited on bushes ten metres or more above the autumn water line, that this now gentle, shallow river became a torrent in the wet season. It is an area of contrasts where little rain falls during the summer, but high precipitation occurs here and in the Genoa's headwaters in winter and spring.

Apart from an occasional lace-monitor on the dry slopes above the river and the much smaller water dragon, *Physignathus lesueurei,* which quickly dived under water as we approached, we saw few reptiles. This was in contrast to an earlier trip to the middle reaches of the Genoa one summer, when we encountered large numbers of active, but extremely shy black snakes. The only other occasion on which I had encountered such numbers of this jet black snake with a contrasting red or cream belly was at Nadgee on the southern New South Wales coast. I have come across this snake more often than any other, but even though they are very venomous, I have never been in a position where I felt in danger of being attacked. On the other hand, no venomous snake should be taken lightly, as they are at their most dangerous when cornered or during the mating season.

One could return time and again to the Genoa River and its surrounding forests and sandstone escarpment, and each time have the thrill of new discoveries. This remote, restful area must still contain many undiscovered fossil records in its ancient rocks. Those that have been found have already supplied a few more pieces to the jig-saw puzzle of the evolution of life on this planet.

11 RIVERINA REMINISCENCES

NEW SOUTH WALES

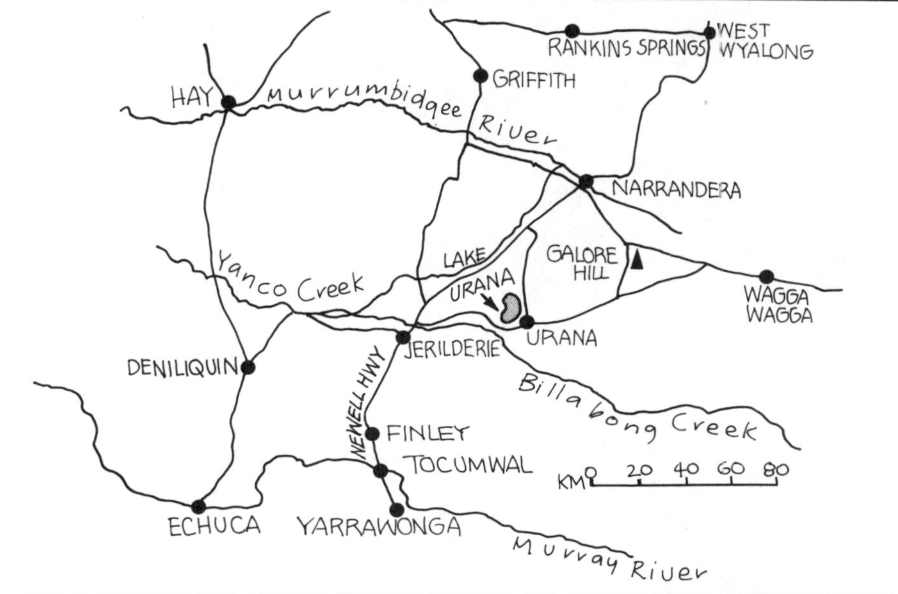

It can often be disillusioning to revisit, in later life, places where you had spent part of your impressionable youth. I used to recall as exciting and romantic the times I had spent in my late-teens working in shearing sheds and on properties in various parts of the southern states. These experiences formed much of the basis of my present philosophies – and I suppose were part of an educational process I had to go through. Now I am anything but proud of my happy participation in the regular slaughter of hundreds of kangaroos – and it is indelibly imprinted on my memory.

At that time, in early post-war Australia, demand from overseas for our wool had pushed the price of top fleece to 'a pound a pound'; an unbelievable price to the farmers who, only a year previously, would have considered a sixth of this as the going price. An immediate response to this bonanza was to find ways to run more sheep on a given area of land. Heavier fertiliser programmes were employed, and grasses and fodder, such as rape seed, sown. The kangaroos, finding this to their liking, immediately increased their breeding levels and the landowners reacted savagely.

Regularly, the district men, with trucks and guns, would descend on a particular property. Up to fifty shooters would station themselves along both fences in the corner of a paddock. The trucks, with horns blaring, would drive the 'roos towards the corner from the far side of the paddock, a distance of a kilometre or more. To a sixteen-year-old, the sight of hundreds of these animals bounding toward their fate was exhilarating; and I was a willing party to the mass slaughterings which were the inevitable consequence. As a devoted animal lover, I still felt no guilt for my part in this destruction: it was my job.

Billabong River

Now, some thirty years on, I revisit these broad plains, now all but devoid of kangaroos. I am well aware of the conflict that once existed, and the often stated argument: 'There were only small mobs of 'roos when white men settled this land. It was the crops he planted for his sheep that allowed them to breed excessively. Shooting them only reduced them to what they originally were.' But my involvement with the slaughter still fills me with disgust.

As I drive through this country there are pleasant things to recall: being shown by an Aboriginal stockman (one of the few in this area) how to detect the holes of true witchetty grubs at the base of a *Eucalyptus camaldulensis* on the banks of the Yanco Creek; and how, by bringing the heel of your hand sharply down on the hole, you could detect by the sound whether the hole had a resident or not. I know, too, that if I walked along this creek (which in flood was many kilometres wide) late on a foggy winter night the hair on the back of my neck would stand up if a musk duck's call boomed out to me across still waters - the call that many believed was emitted by the mythical bunyip.

It was only recently that I read of palaeobotanical studies that revealed pollen samples of an ancient ilex (holly) species from deep below the present flat plain: an indicator that this was once an area carrying lush rainforest plants.

Like the earlier childhood experiences in the quarries and on the rivers and plains around my home, these later experiences gave me a feel for my country that no amount of schooling could do. I was learning empirically, and I was a willing student.

On the many properties throughout southern Australia on which I worked, I met people who seemed to have an affinity with the land — but none of this comprised a sense of husbandry. It was always, what can we get out of it, rather than how can we care for it? They saw the land as capable of endless exploitation — strip one area, then another: 'She's a big country, and there's plenty more!'

Nature works on a vast time scale; man modifies or destroys in minutes. As keepers, not owners, of this vast heritage, we need to beware of any actions that may irreversibly damage the environment and snap the thread of evolution. Only an understanding of the frail elements that comprise this great land can teach us to understand how to live more harmoniously with it, both for its sake and our own.

12 MAJOR SANDSTONE FLORAL AREAS

VICTORIA NEW SOUTH WALES & WESTERN AUSTRALIA

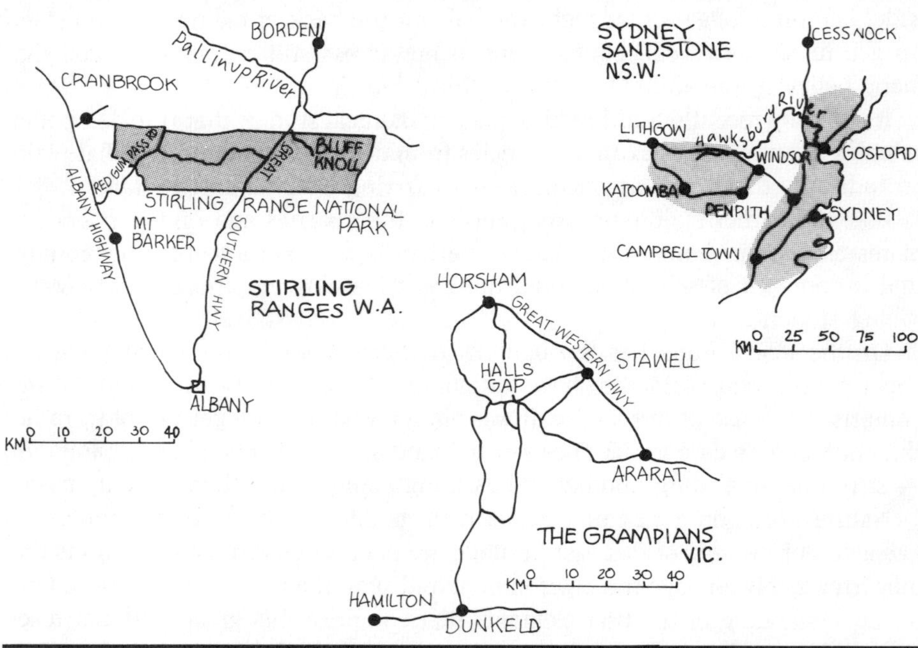

The major floristic sandstone areas in southern Australia are the Grampians in western Victoria, the Stirlings in Western Australia, and the Hawkesbury plateau of Sydney. None of these is of great elevation or extent; but on their ridges and slopes and in their valleys grow some of the most beautiful and rare plants to be found in any of the three states.

As an example, the Grampians, a series of ranges running approximately north and south for 90 kilometres, contains around one-third of the naturally growing plants of Victoria – this in an area less than 1 per cent of the total area of the state. Of around 1000 different species of plants, more than twenty are found nowhere else; they are endemic to this limited area. This is a very old mountain system which originated as warped, uplifted and weathered sediments, laid down in a vast lake system approximately 400 000 000 years ago.

The steep easterly scarps and gradual western flanks bear little resemblance today to the roller-coaster contours that were the Grampians of long ago. Rain, wind, sun, and ice have all played their part in the relentless reshaping of this ancient landform, and the Pliocene seas lapped around its base as recently as 3 000 000 years ago. It was in such isolation that new plants evolved from ancient, widespread stock, or local pressures either eliminated or placed other species in positions where dramatic change in their appearance took place.

That is why, when we now visit similar rock structures, even though they may be hundreds, or even thousands of kilometres apart and separated by dissimilar environments, we can find the same species, or some which have obviously derived from a common stock.

In the Grampians, for instance, there is a grevillea, *G. dimorpha*, which is currently considered to be endemic to these ranges. It is obviously closely related to two further species, *G. oleoides* and *G. speciosa*, both of which occur only on the sandstone around Sydney, or in the Blue Mountains, in heathland, dry forests, or in the case of *G. oleoides*, on creek banks around the Sutherland waterfall area. These are the sorts of habitats favoured by *G. dimorpha* in the eastern ranges of the Grampians. Even in such a restricted area of occurrence, there is such variation in the size and shape of leaves from one population to another, that the uninitiated could be forgiven in thinking they were looking at more than one species. *Grevillea parvifolia* is a further species which occurs in both localities as well as through Gippsland, and in drier areas of Victoria, sometimes on the mallee margins. On exposed rocks above the Hawkesbury River and in grasslands of the Brisbane Ranges, north of Geelong in Victoria, this narrow-leaved plant can be a wiry subshrub no more than a few centimetres high; whereas on creeksides such as Currumbene Creek, south of Nowra in New South Wales, it can be a tall shrub of two metres with arching branches. What the ancestors of all these plants looked like, and where they first colonised, is uncertain; what we can say with some certainty, is that favourable sites were invaded by these ancestors while Australia was still attached to Antarctica. These ancestors, known as Gondwana flora, moved across the landmass formed by today's South America, Africa, India, and New Zealand via Australia, providing the basis from which separate evolutionary paths began. These ancient links can still be traced in the extant flora of all these now far-flung continents.

To illustrate these links, no more widespread or diversely beautiful family than the Proteaceae could be chosen. South Africa, in particular the Cape Province, is renowned for its dominant genera of *Protea*, *Leucospermum* and *Leucadendron*. Australia's fame for flowers of this nature centres around *Banksia*, *Telopea*, or *Grevillea*, the three better-known members of the family in the two eastern sandstone centres.

In Western Australia, the Stirlings are the home of other members of the family. Petrophiles and Isopogons, both of which are also found in the east, reach a high level of development and diversity here. *Isopogon latifolius* is the most spectacular of these, and is found clinging to the upper western slopes. The flower heads resemble deep pink mop heads, which gives rise to the common name of 'pixie mops'. The genus *Dryandra* evolved many of its species in and around these confined but majestic ranges, which were cut off from transcontinental plant movement as recently as 25 million years ago by the advent of the Nullarbor Plain, and by vast seas that lapped at their flanks many times during their history. Dryandras, while closely related to banksias, which are found Australia-wide, occur only in Western Australia. Of the more than 60 species, *Dryandra formosa* is one of the most outstanding. *Dryandra formosa's* foliage is soft and finely divided, unlike that of many species whose rigid leaves create an almost impenetrable barrier (for all but small birds and animals) to the flowers hidden away in the centre of the bush. Its adaptability is seen by the diversity of habitat it occupies. Down on the plains, in view of Bluff Knoll, the highest peak at 1100 metres in this rugged range, it grows as an open shrub, with the large golden bunches of flowers thrusting out and up at the ends of the branches.

Bluff Knoll

Many of the spectacular, nectar-bearing plants have evolved flowers so positioned and so colourful that they are sure to attract their fair share of the pollinating agents. These may be birds, or insects, and in some instances, small honeyeating possums, whose tongues and snouts have also adapted to provide more efficient tools for nectar extraction.

The relationship between plants, birds, insects, and animals so often clearly illustrates the time scale involved to produce such extraordinarily efficient relationships. It is easy to take all this for granted. But it is important to understand the vast time scale involved, and the amount of trial and error that has produced what we now see. We don't see or often even know of the plants that no longer exist because they found the competition for a limited site too tough, or perhaps because of a reduction in rainfall. Fossils of plants and animals, often found in coal deposits and limestone, bear testimony to those that found change too difficult to cope with.

If we travel to the eastern freeboard of the continent, taking perhaps two days to cross the barriers of the Nullarbor, the rivers and deserts and mountain ranges, we may find ourselves standing on another vast sandstone plateau which, unlike the Grampians or the Stirlings, stretches as far as one can see. This is what is loosely known as the Hawkesbury sandstone, a name taken from the major waterway that cuts deeply into this relatively low mass of rock.

This and surrounding similar sandstone areas occupy about 3 per cent of the area of New South Wales, which is considered to be the most floristically diverse of all states. With a total of approximately 6000 species of plants, it is only slightly behind Western Australia, which is vastly bigger and referred to as 'the wildflower State'. In NSW, however, this number of plants is shared amongst a greater diversity of habitats: rainforest, sclerophyll forest, desert, sand heaths, and the highest alpine region in the continent.

Within the concentrated diversity and beauty of the sandstone areas grow about 10 per cent of the state's total plants. Growing in an area where the coarse rock has weathered to sand and blended with decomposing leaves and twigs to form soil only inches deep, are boronias, eriostemons, grevilleas, epacris, actinotus, and other smaller plants – truly a wildflower garden. Boronias and other members of the Rutaceae family, correas, eriostemons, and croweas, have reached a high level of development in these shallow infertile soils. The profusion of these, and the attendant diversity of other small and large plants, clearly illustrates how successfully they have adjusted to soils leached of all but the minimum of sustenance.

The Hawkesbury differs from the Grampians or Stirlings in having extensive waterways leading into the ocean. Because of the formation of this plateau – which was uplifted slowly from an inundated basin in a vertical structure – weaknesses and faults were quickly eroded by water; and over a period of 200 000 000 years this has etched out such extensive rivers as the Hawkesbury. To travel this waterway by boat is to discover more about the flora.

The creamy twisted trunks of *Angophora costata*, whose roots grasp tenuously at cracks in the rock shelves, seem to balance precariously on the edges of sheer drops above the water. When one examines them closely, and sees the almost foot-like flanges spreading across the rock from their trunks to provide additional support, one recognises how secure and permanent a part of this panorama they are.

The fact that, even with these vast differences in distance, we can see clear floral links illustrates just how widespread and continuous the flora must once have been and how immense the time scale involved.

13 AT MY BACK DOOR

VICTORIA

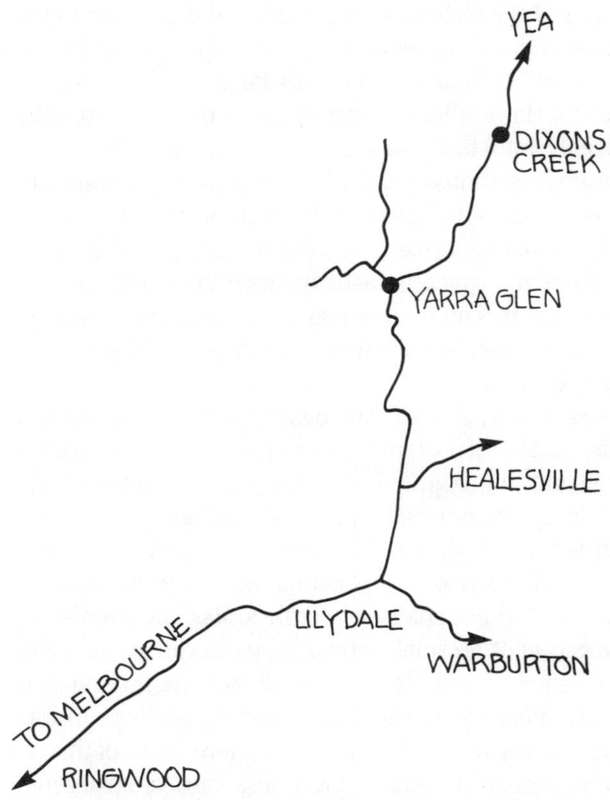

For many people wildflowers conjure up a vision of childhood wanderings through bushland, collecting and making a bouquet of small flowers. Before the war such patches of bushland were very close to the city, but now suburban development has taken over most of the open forest woodland.

It is pleasantly surprising how much can still be found right in the heart of heavily populated areas. Railway embankments and reserves throughout Australia still carry plants much as they did before the city's growth. Two Melbourne areas, between Heathmont and Bayswater and along the Ringwood-East Ringwood railway line, are favourite haunts of local wildflower enthusiasts, with small terrestrial orchids being of particular interest. These have to be carefully watched for, since they often grow in grass tufts or leaf litter and are difficult to spot.

Lately I have been driving through the back of Park Orchards on the way to Templestowe. On a particular day a light haze of blue flowers caught my eye, and I wondered why I hadn't seen them the week before. There were so many they would surely have been impossible to miss. A quick stop and inspection revealed why. The flowers belonged to *Dichopogon strictus*, a lily plant widespread throughout temperate eastern Australia which bears the common name of chocolate lily, because of a light perfume from the flowers. Its flowers are held on fine stems about 45 centimetres above the foliage, which is often below field grass level, and they open quickly and in profusion. They are pale lilac to blue and their 'not here one minute – here the next' style can come as a pleasant surprise. It is not every year that they flower in such profusion; ideal seasonal conditions are needed to allow the species to fulfil its potential, and if an attempt is made to grow it in cultivation, an open, well-drained site must be chosen.

This plant ties together a wildflower kaleidoscope that we recently found again in the Chiltern State Forest. (I have known this area for many years, mainly because of an unusual form of *Grevillea alpina*.) But never have I seen it as on this day. As well as chocolate lily, which made a filmy mist above the ground, another lily, *Burchardia umbellata* paraded through clumps of poa at no more than a few centimetres above ground level, although occasional plants were nearly 30 centimetres high. This dainty plant bears the common name of milkmaids, perhaps an allusion, with its white-banded flowers, to our storybook image of milkmaids' skirts. It has a delicate perfume.

Three other members of the Liliaceae family sharing the space were *Bulbine bulbosa*, *Dianella revoluta* and *Dianella laevis*. The first is a small fine-stemmed herb that grows to about 30 centimetres with bright yellow flowers, and it was named bulbine lily or native leek by early settlers. The second two, which fall into the group of flax lilies owing to their upright strap-like leaves, are hardy plants that have not attained the horticultural acceptance they deserve. There are four species of *Dianella* in Victoria, all with deep blue flowers with yellow centres. The petals shine as if enamelled and the racemes are always prominently displayed above the flax-like leaves. Terrestrial orchids grow through the forest in profusion and care has to be taken not to tread on them.

Other plants in this wildflower carpet included masses of pea flowers. These commonly come under the mantle of egg and bacon – another early settlers' name alluding to the bright yellow and often brown tints of the flowers. *Dillwynia retorta*, *Dillwynia sericea* (both small soft shrubs to 60 centimetres) and *Pultenaea pedunculata* (a dense suckering mat) were the most prolific species. Helichrysums (the everlastings) were in field-like proportions of gold, with the fine-leafed *Helichrysum bracteatum* and *Helichrysum semipapposum*, together with *Helipterum albicans*, glowing and silver-foliaged, almost blanketing out any other plants. Further yellow and gold was supplied by *Acacia aculeatissima*, often growing at ground level with *Goodenia pinnatifida* and *Goodenia lanata*, while above them the fine-foliaged *Gompholobium huegelii* sported large pea flowers.

A number of these plants grow virtually at my back door – or, rather, a short walk into the dry sclerophyll forests from my back door. Just last weekend, in early November, when I was walking my dogs along a rough forest track, one which I had not been on for many months, I started seeing small plants I hadn't remembered from last year or the year before.

Xanthorrhoea minor is a small grass tree which, unlike many species, has an underground trunk, with just a few long rigid leaves above ground. Here it had produced masses of highly scented white heads of minute lilies, six or more stems apparently from each plant. The flower heads were about 15 centimetres long, borne on the end of bare stalks nearly 90 centimetres tall. As if to illustrate that I hadn't been unobservant on previous walks, the following week colonies of them were flowering on the road verges running beside local horse studs.

Competing with them for sheer purity of colour was a dwarf form of *Leptospermum juniperinum*. This slightly prickly foliaged shrub can grow to more than 2 metres, but none in my area is taller than 1 metre, and most plants are much shorter. The clean white flowers are produced along the full length of the stems, thereby smothering the plant when they are fully open. Very occasionally a plant will have pink buds, and this introduces a subtlety of tone to a drift of otherwise white flower.

Although not in flower, large shrubs of *Banksia spinulosa* were prominent on the sides of gullies. This is close to the western limits of occurrence for this species, with populations at Kinglake and Montrose being the extremes. This well-known large shrub was also recorded from Mt Richmond near Portland in the Western District of Victoria, but that record has since proven to be a misidentification of *Banksia marginata*.

When we first purchased our four-acre cow paddock, a role it had served since probably 1920 or earlier, there was not a tree left on it. My vision was to create a large part of it as a deep water area, for bird habitat, and for the tranquillity water always offers. I spent nearly two years testing soil, taking levels, and generally developing a feeling of how the lake should look.

Just four years ago, a team of bulldozers under my guidance, created the area which now holds one and a half million gallons of water. Some of the soil that came from the excavation was used to create a small island, intended as a breeding area for birds, and the balance was used to contour low profile hills throughout the remaining three acres.

So there we were, with a large yellow hole in the ground containing a pool of muddy water in the bottom; not very impressive at that stage. Grassing all banks and slopes, and planting the island with melaleucas, callistemons, leptospermums and hakeas were the first steps in the second stage, that of turning this future lake into a living environment. With that done, rushes were scrounged from nearby ponds, as were a few plants of *Ottelia ovalifolia*, a floating water plant with purple-centred yellow flowers.

The rains came and she was full to the brim! In fact, the lake could have filled ten times over with the amount of winter rain we had in 1981, the year before the drought. So then we watched it develop. Our grass sprouted, our yellow mounds became green contours and part of the local landscape; the rushes grew, and suddenly the first waterbirds started to arrive.

It was a time of excitement and constant expectation. One morning we found a pair of swans gracefully gliding across the still water. Sadly, it was not to their liking and away they flew. But in that first year we recorded twelve different species of waterbird. For the next two years this number stabilised. Though black ducks would not breed here, they did so in smaller, more enclosed ponds next door, then immediately transferred their broods to our larger water for training. One lone eastern swamp-hen would spend a few days on the island, then disappear; obviously the habitat was not to her liking.

In the past twelve months the rushes and reeds have surrounded the lake's waterline; the *Ottelia*, from one lone plant, is now sheeting large areas of the shallow water; and the island is a dense thicket more than three metres high.

Suddenly, as if by magic, we now have numerous pairs of eastern swamp-hen, dusky moorhen, and the white-browed coot; as well as two species of grebe building nests and platforms wherever a clump of *Juncus* or *Eleocharis* is of sufficient size. Plover, wood duck, mountain duck, heron, and even a rare garganey teal, are regular or occasional visitors.

Our lake has come of age; it has matured to a point where these diverse birds now feel at home. Before our eyes, we have seen the importance of habitat for such waterbirds. It has been a graphic lesson to us.

Banksia laracina

14 CLOSE TO HOME

GEORGES RIVER NEW SOUTH WALES

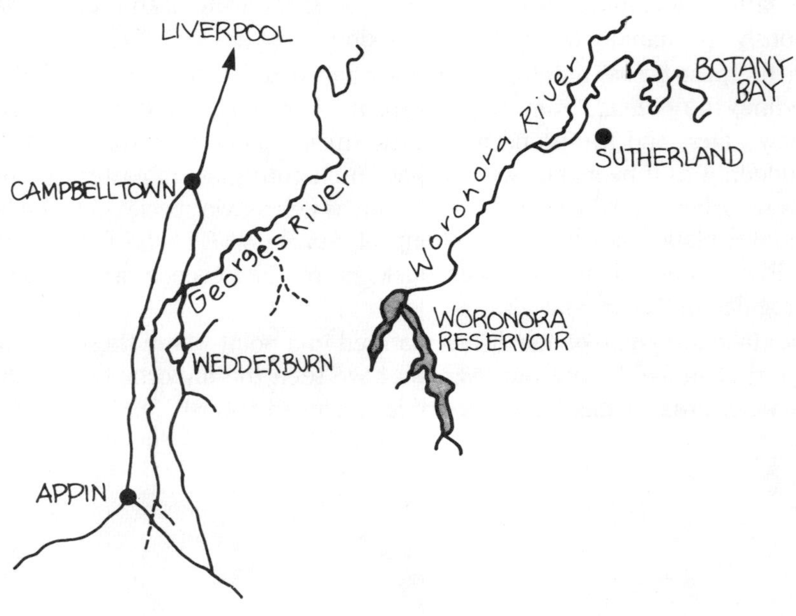

Most major Australian capital cities have interesting areas of flora within a short driving time of suburbia. Perth has much to offer. Less than an hour from the city centre, at Lesmurdie Falls in the Darling Ranges, an outstanding array of wildflowers exists. From Melbourne, in just over an hour, you can be at Toolangi amidst massive *Nothofagus* or 'beech' and dense moist fern gullies. From Hobart, in the same time, you can be on top of Mt Wellington with its dwarfed alpine environment. The northern sandstone plateaus of Sydney carry a wonderful array of plants; but it was only recently that I came across an unexpected area of great interest, south-west of that city.

It is the sandstone country through which the headwaters of the Georges River cut, and only a few minutes drive from Campbelltown, which sits on the extensive clay plain covering much of this country. I had driven through here often, unaware that, cutting into this yellow-red clay, the Georges River has created a small gorge that carries an array of flora as extensive as that on the northern sandstone plateaus.

I had dropped down into the gorge on the road leading to a property I was to visit at Wedderburn, and the change was dramatic.

The first impression as I descended was of the sandstone shelving, sculpturally worn, which replaced the flat clay plain above; and then of the liane-like festooning of trees by *Clematis glycinoides* in full bloom. This change from the dry sclerophyll aspect of the eucalyptus forest above to the remnant rainforest around the water occurs not infrequently through the Sydney area, but it is none the less startling. This *Clematis* species is a dainty plant, smaller in leaf, flower, and possibly in general size, than the more familiar *C. aristata*. The flowers are the same satin-sheen white, and covered the climbing stems with their fine-petalled mass.

It is obvious that a few dominant flowering plants will catch your attention when you enter new or unexpected areas; and such was the case with *Eriostemon australasius*. Its creamy white to deep pink waxy flowers studded the backdrop of grey-green foliage like so many transfixed butterflies. On closer examination it is easy to see how the common name 'wax flower' is derived. Unlike the filmy fine petals of the clematis, those on the eriostemon are thick and stiff, giving the appearance of having been moulded from pink wax. Most of the shrubs were less than a metre in height, and no two plants displayed flowers of the same colouring. *Eriostemon australasius* flowers over a long period, from early to late spring, and new buds, flowers and developing seed capsules were present on all plants.

As I worked up the slopes onto the drier shelves, other plants which formed this rich heathland begged attention. None in flower presented the vast numbers of the eriostemon, but a large number formed a mosaic of subtle colour and tone. Yellow was present in one of the 'true butterflies' of the plant world, *Gompholobium grandiflorum*, a waist-high shrub with narrow leaflets and large bright pea flowers. Deep purple-blue was present on the furry grey stems of *Dampiera purpurea*, which looks almost black in bud, so dense are the dark grey flowers. Many dampieras are compact, trailing or mounding plants but this species mostly comprises a few erect stems to more than a metre tall, a structure which is striking in a garden situation. Like many wild flowers, this one has been successfully tamed.

Another two pea-flowered plants, both dillwynias, and not as structurally dominant as the gompholobium, have a fine appearance, a small stature, and yellow and red flowers, variously displayed on or at the ends of branches. These two, *D. glaberrima* and *D. parvifolia* are, like many of their family, attractive to butterflies, which transfer pollen from one plant to another.

Pimelea linifolia,too, attracts butterflies to its pom-pom heads of cream flowers, an arrangement which the majority of species in this widespread family share. One exception is *P. axiflora*, a fine weeping shrub of 2 metres, found in moist mountain areas of NSW, Victoria and Tasmania. This species has the toughest of fibrous bark on its small trunks, and gained its common name 'bootlace bush' from the use of its bark by woodcutters and bushmen for that purpose. The flowers in this instance are in groups and sit in the joints made by stem and leaf stalk.

As in many heathland areas of southern Australia, the family Proteaceae is well represented. Here on the sandstone, three grevilleas, two isopogons, two banksias, one conospermum, one lambertia, and two persoonias, illustrate the diversity which has evolved in this widespread family. The three grevilleas, *G. cinerea*, *G. parviflora*, and *G. sphacelata*, illustrate this as well as any genus. *G. cinerea* is a rounded shrub, with soft, hairy rounded leaves and large individual green flowers from which protrudes a red style. These flowers, tucked away in similar coloured leaves, produce copious quantities of rich nectar that attracts the birds to their hiding place. *Grevillea parviflora* is quite open in habit, with narrow leaves and umbels of individually small white or pink flowers. It is a species confined to NSW and Victoria, and varies as greatly in habit and size as it does in habitat. It may occupy moist creeksides, where it is a graceful weeping shrub to 2 metres, as well as dry grasslands, where at 5 centimetres high it takes some finding in the grass.

Wildflower selection: 1 *Acacia terminalis* 2 *Grevillea buxifolia* 3 *Hakea dactyloides* 4 *Mirbelia rubiifolia* 5 *Boronia serrulata* 6 *Dampiera purpurea* 7 *Lambertia formosa* 8 *Eriostemon australasius* 9 *Isopogon anemonifolius* (centre)

I use all of these forms in any landscape design work that calls for fine, subtle texture. The third is *G. sphacelata* (which derives from the Greek for gangrene). Like many plants, it bears a name the beholder may find obscure – and a little unfortunate. In this instance, the scholarly Robert Brown evidently considered that the unusual colour of the flower, a combination of grey, pink and a little brown, reminded him of the tonings of a gangrenous wound he had had the misfortune to witness. It hardly does justice to this attractive small shrub a metre tall, with fine hairy leaves. The flowers, in a spidery cluster held upright at the ends of stems, are quite attractive.

There are only four species of *Grevillea* with this floral structure. Three of them grow around Sydney, *G. buxifolia* being the better known in horticulture, *G. phylicoides* little known. The fourth, *G. occidentalis*, grows in Western Australia – a separate accidental development, or a long-distance relative?

Another puzzler is that there is only one species of *Lambertia* in eastern Australia, and this one, *L. formosa*, is confined to an area of New South Wales which is mainly sandstone in structure. It is open in habit, up to about 2 metres tall, with bright orange/red upright tubular flowers. The seed capsules are a quaint shape, looking like miniature Satans, hence the popular name 'mountain devil'. *Lambertia* has its major development in Western Australia, where approximately eight species grow in not dissimilar habitats.

Most people with some awareness of plants can look at members of the Proteaceae family and detect a relationship. *Conospermum*, though, always seems to me to be the odd man out. Only a small number of species occur on the eastern freeboard, but there are more than thirty in Western Australia, where they are commonly called 'smoke bush', and very aptly so for many species. *C. stoechadis* can grow in a large community and the masses of smokey grey-white flowers, individually small, look from a distance like a low-hanging drift of smoke. Other species, which may be blue, white or grey/blue, impart their own impression of a smoke screen.

The species I found at Georges River was *C. longifolium*, which has erect strap-like leaves arising from a common base, and pale flowers on stalks above the foliage.

As I wandered further into this country – involved to the point where I was almost able to ignore the piles of household refuse, car parts, and old furniture that had been dumped in 'the scrub' – I started to look into the mid and upper storey, which provided the canopy for this landscape. As is so often the case in these sandstone outcrops, the smooth pink to orange trunks of *Angophora costata* were visually the most appealing; the more sombre *Eucalyptus gummifera*, one of the 'bloodwoods' and a prolifically flowering tree, was no less beautiful though, with its flaking small shields of bark, and umbrageous canopy. Sharing a crowded habitat and more variable in size was *Eucalyptus punctata*, locally called grey gum. It is variable because soil depth affects its shape markedly. On the sandstone shelves its white-grey trunks are often twisted, as are some branches, and its stature quite small; while in deeper soil near by it is a tall straight-trunked tree with a definite stocking of dark bark at the base. Often breaking the line of the trunks of trees were two medium acacias, with distinctively different foliage and floral arrangements.

Acacia longissima is a strong component of the shallow soils of sandstone shelves. It has an open soft arching habit, the leaves are fine and simple, the flowers cream-yellow, and they appear at different times throughout the year. *A. terminalis*, which is the unfortunate recipient of many name changes, has broad shiny pinnate leaves, the new growth of which varies from gold to red. It is the racemes of bright yellow flowers held above the leaves which give rise to its common name of sunshine wattle. Whilst not many were in flower, those that were lit up the dappled shade with their brightness. Beneath the acacias, *Thelymitra media*, a beautiful blue to purple flowered sun orchid, was only 30 centimetres high, with flowers crowded up the upright stems. Often beside these was an unusual trigger-plant or *Stylidium*, *S. laricifolia*, which is one of the tallest and longest-leaved members of a mostly herbaceous family. The specific name *laricifolia* is an evident allusion to the northern hemisphere larch, since the leaves are long and fine and arranged in groups around the upright stems. This finely structured plant is known only from one area in Victoria around Wingan Inlet, and having seen it there beside the track above the camping area, I don't recall that it was as large as its Sydney counterpart.

I had reached a clearing which bordered bare shelves of sandstone jutting out into space above the Georges River. I sat for some time listening to a gaggle of friar-birds feeding on blossoms near by, and enjoyed the vista down into the river valley.

I know of many such beautiful places around Sydney where, only a few minutes from main thoroughfares, you can sit as I did and look upon almost untrodden bushland. We are indeed fortunate to have this space and freedom often remarked on by many overseas people, from countries where such natural tracts so close to major cities no longer exist.

Eucalyptus coronata

15 THE GRAMPIANS

VICTORIA

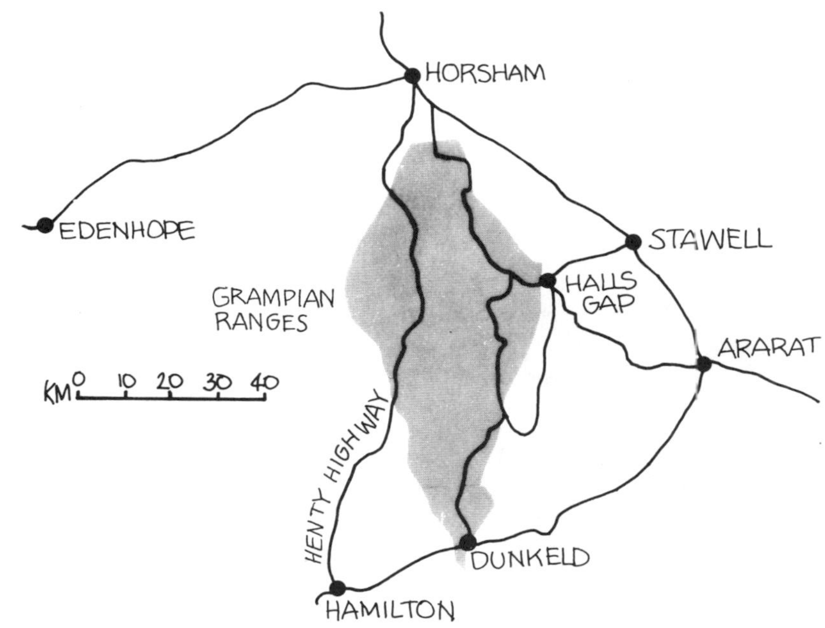

The Grampians conjure up scenes of steeply sloping sandstone ranges. From the roads that wind through them you see dwarfed growth on the drier exposed sides, and in the shelter and shade provided by many of the hills the myriad creeks support lush populations of shade-dwelling plants. But where the ranges suddenly plunge into the earth, and lightly undulating farm and forest land move westward, a new environment appears, one in which many feel far more comfortable than in dense bushland. It is easy to walk through, under the widely spaced broad-canopied trees. Here *Eucalyptus melliodora* (the yellow box) and *Eucalyptus camaldulensis* (the river red gum) indicate by their positions those sites better drained or slightly wetter.

A flash of colour signals the movement of a rainbow bird through the lower branches; swallows wheel in insect-searching flights; rosellas voice their pleasure at finding trees in blossom. Sharing this feast, numbers of small honeyeaters, often with calls deceptively loud for their size, dart inquiringly from their feeding to inspect intruders walking through their domain.

The light, only occasional one dull day when I was there , picks up the feathery heads of grasses and sedges that are the linking theme of the low heathland. There is no clutter here, and even though a hundred small species of plants dot the ground a relaxing sense of space is felt. Guinea flowers, in the form of *Hibbertia sericea* – small, mounded and silky grey; *Hibbertia fasciculata* with tight bundles of leaves on upright stems; and the rare prostrate *Hibbertia humifusa;* all with their buttercup yellow flowers: these show how the Australian bush can surprise where surprise is not expected. The ability of one plant to complement another has prompted the often-heard statement that the bush has a sameness. But you have only to look, and the flower draws attention to the subtleties of each one.

All these wildflowers are found at the Grampians: 1 *Caladenia patersonii* 2 *Epacris impressa* 3 *Caleana major* 4 *Hakea rostrata* 5 *Styphelia adscendens* 6 *Stypandra glauca* 7 *Sprengelia incarnata* 8 *Thryptomene calycina* 9 *Correa aemula* 10 *Grevillea aquifolium*

Ancient grass trees, *Xanthorrhoea australis*, were in full flower, long thick stalks supporting thousands of flowers thrust skyward from the skirt of leaves. From a distance these flower spikes appear as a white mass up to 2 metres high. A close inspection reveals that thousands of individual flowers (actually lilies) are inserted into the stalk. Their perfume and nectar ensure a constant supply of birds – and the beetles which, in their clumsy tramplings, take pollen from flower to flower are one of the main sources of transference. Smaller lilies, the white heads of *Burchardia* and the blue of *Dichopogon*, accompany the grasses and herbs. Careful placement of each footstep is necessary to ensure minimum damage to these and the fine-stemmed ground orchids, many only a few centimetres high.

Drier slopes are like a sombre artist's pallette, relieved by the random splashes of matted bush pea, *Pultenaea pedunculata*. 'Mat' describes them well, as they may rise only fractionally above the stony gravel, spreading like a mat and displaying orange-red or yellow pea flowers up to 3 centimetres above the foliage.

The singular white purity of silky tea-tree, *Leptospermum myrsinoides*, ties much of this theme together, drawing the eye farther into the distance. This is one of the drier area tea-trees; and where seasonal moisture collects this gives way to prickly or black tea-tree, *Leptospermum juniperinum*. Here the yellow matting, *Goodenia geniculata*, favouring sandy gravel soils, is replaced by the even brighter yellow of *Ranunculus robertsoniana*, a buttercup species.

The object in landscape gardening is to capture and recreate the feeling of openness in a narrow landscape, to simulate this on a small scale. Simulation I consider to be a key to what we may hope to achieve in capturing the simpler essence of natural landscape.

However sympathetically approached, many potentially good landscapes do not attain the effect aimed at. With all the effort and consideration given to use of rocks, gravels, mounds and logs, it is finally in the selection of plants that the landscape is completed.

I thought as I walked through this woodland, with sedges and small plants flicking my feet, of the greater illusion of space the small landscape could offer with even small open areas simply planted with this material.

Near Redman's Bluff, while experiencing similar pleasures, Sue and I were making our way down a slope where *Eucalyptus ovata* was the dominant tree. Suddenly the warm eucalypt and forest smell was temporarily replaced by a much muskier smell. Immediately I said, 'There's a koala near by.' My childhood memory of that smell is deeply embedded in my olfactory recording system. Sure enough, high in the fork of a tree above us, sat a lone koala, which responded to our calls merely with a brief sleepy look before resuming his sleep. From his high perch his urine sprays down onto lower leaves and it is this which permeates the area with its muskiness.

Similar strong impressions from childhood bush experiences flood back whenever I am in dense moist forests, such as Sherbrooke near Melbourne. I am seldom tricked by the mimicry of the lyrebird as it impersonates the other birds of the forest. There is a purity in its tone which outdoes the original songbird; but it is the lyrebird's ability to run through its repertoire without a break which is the giveaway. Grey thrush, currawong, crimson rosellas in flocks, gang-gang, tree-creeper and kookaburra are all part of his continuous concert. His own rapid *click-click*, with his magnificent tail fanned overhead, quivering as he jumps and hops, is pure music and movement. Just as expected, as the flowers I know I will find in bloom, is the plaintive, yet musical call of the currawong during summertime, high in the alpine areas of Victoria and New South Wales, or among the forests and heathlands of the Hawkesbury, near Sydney.

Being involved with nature is a very personal experience, and no doubt we all perceive it in different ways. The relationship between rock and soil, soil and plants, and between plants and birds and animals, has evolved on a time scale almost too vast to comprehend. All have their parts to play, and all have their meaning; and understanding this is perhaps the greatest difficulty man encounters.

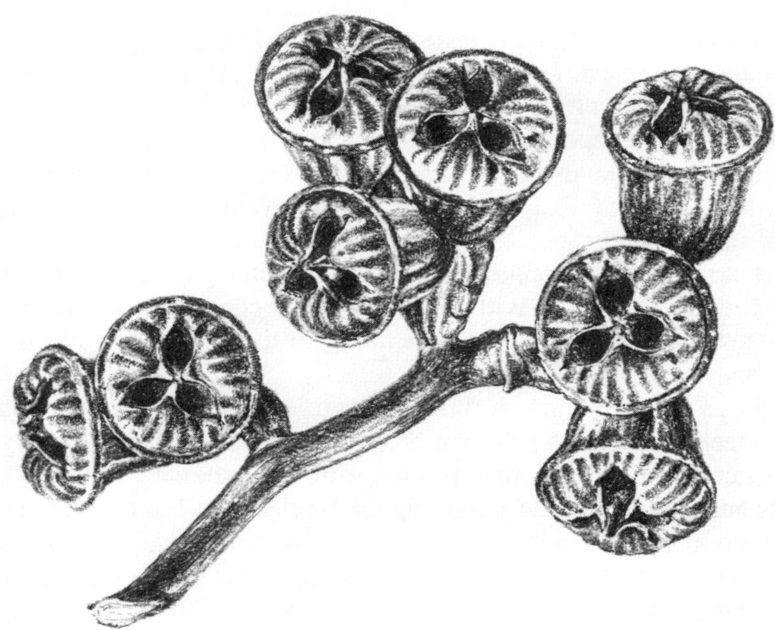

Eucalyptus burdettiana

16 NORTHERN TERRITORY

THE KIMBERLEYS I WESTERN AUSTRALIA

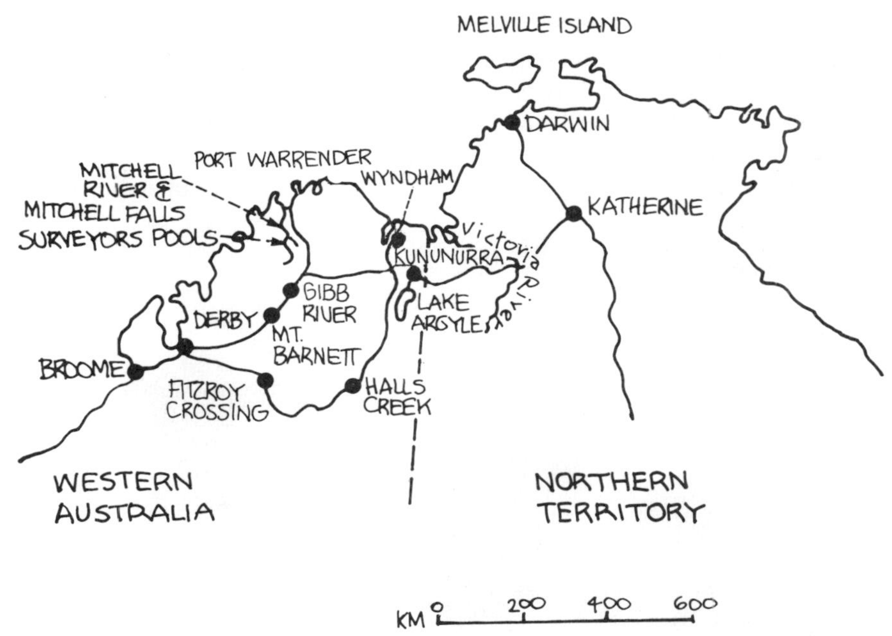

A postponed overseas trip in 1982, for which we had allowed five weeks, gave us the opportunity to explore the top north-western corner of Australia. It was country I had not visited, but Sue had spent some time there ten years previously.

We planned to fly to Darwin, collect an off-road hire vehicle, and travel west into Western Australia. Once there, it was our intention to skirt the northern Kimberley, then head due north to the Mitchell River area, as by June most of the swollen rivers would have dropped, allowing easy crossing.

Our vehicle, which looked as if it had just completed an around-Australia endurance test, was waiting at the Darwin Airport. It had a disturbing lean at the left back, even without any cargo, and the tyres, all five of them, had only the final thin layer of tread left. Since we were about to embark on a 5000 kilometre jaunt into remote and rough country, I persuaded the hire company to put five new tyres on, and wire down a few other loose odds and ends. The lean didn't appear as bad with new tyres, not until we loaded the boxes containing our gear into the back. We had booked the vehicle six months previously, and I had built and forwarded to Darwin boxes that fitted neatly into the space between the wheel humps. Dubious as we were, we took off, heading south on the road to Katherine.

The country around Darwin is mostly flat and generally black. This comes about through an almost permanent Northern Territory habit of grass-burning. It is done to clear land, control weeds, and herd cattle; so even in the most remote areas you will often drive through palls of smoke, mile after mile, or come across grass fires on road verges. Seldom do you see people in attendance, as most of the fires are set by aeroplane drops, or lit by hand and then abandoned.

I was not prepared for the generally sclerophyll nature of the vegetation through which we travelled on our way to Kununurra, gateway to the Kimberley. Even with a tropical summer rainfall, and high temperatures and humidity, only patches of tropical vegetation exist. These patches are more in the nature of vine thickets and, as we were to find later in the far north-west, just about impenetrable.

Baobab seed pods: the pods are suitable for carving

The Tasmanian endemic *Diplarrena latifolia,* right: one of the few members of the 'Iris' family in Australia. It is not as widespread as the larger *D. moraea,* which also occurs on the mainland. Below, Lake Pedder before HEC 'improvements'. This beautiful, isolated lake became a martyr to the cause of future conservation action in Tasmania

On the slopes of the ancient sedimentary beds through which the Murchison River cuts, herds of destructive goats graze, and in the valleys the very salty water seems odd in this pristine scene. On the sandy plains above the river, a diverse beautiful flora exists. *Grevillea annulifera,* the medium shrub with bicoloured flowers (left) is a haven for nectar-feeding birds

'I want to take you home', Sue seems to be saying to a 'parent baobab' surrounded by offspring. This bottle-shaped tree, *Adansonia gregorii,* bears large fluffy flowers followed by cricket-ball-sized seed capsules. A close-up of *Cochlospermum fraseri* (right), a small open deciduous tree that bears large yellow flowers when the branches are bare. The common name, Kapok, derives from the hairs surrounding the seeds. Both trees are found in the Kimberleys

Fire often initiates the mass flowering of *Xanthorrhoea australis,* frequently labelled 'Grass Tree' because of its fine foliage. Tall, with weirdly twisted flower stalks comprised of thousands of small cream, highly nectariferous flowers, it is actually a lily which flourishes in sandstone habitats. At left, a coastal form of *Grevillea lanigera,* seen at Singapore Peninsula. Growing in a compact mound almost to the water's edge, it retains this shape in gardens

The most impressive tree, which often occurred in pure stands, was *Adansonia gregorii*, the 'baobab'. It is impressive in all aspects. The shape is distinctive, with a broad swollen base; a classic bottle shape, with the neck removed. Thick angular branches extend from the shoulder of the 'bottle', and these are bare during the wet, then clothed with large, usually radiating leaves, from late summer onwards. We missed the fluffy flowers that follow the wet season, but found any number of the cricket-ball-sized seed pods. These were either still on the tree, hanging on long peduncles, or lying all around the base of the tree. They are actually dark in colour, but a clothing of whitish hair gives them a soft appearance.

We had read that both the seed, and the white pith were edible, and we had no trouble in cracking one open to try. The pith is dry and needed to be chewed in small pieces, and though the taste was pleasantly nutty-sweet we found difficulty in producing enough mouth moisture in the hot conditions to make eating easy.

Dominating the landscape were the 'bloodwood' eucalypts. They are ubiquitous. A number of species have creamy white flowers; a few have bright red or pink massed blooms. The smallest of these is *E. setosa*, which we found on specific soil types right across the top from Darwin to the northern Kimberley. It is not a large tree; in fact, it is more of a large shrub in habit, with rigid hairs on the leaves, stems, and buds, which open into pink flowers. This is the case, too, with *E. ptychocarpa*, a much taller traditionally shaped tree. It was seen only near watercourses; and as these are few and far between throughout much of the north, not many were observed. It was unusual to come across clear-trunked eucalypts, but two were consistent in a range of habitats. The smaller of the two, *E. brevifolia*, usually around 3-4 metres, bore small neat foliage, its trunk and branches heavily powdered with a white bloom. *E. bigalerita* had the most appealing trunk of all that we saw. Its salmon-pink smoothness was reminiscent of *E. salmonophloia*, found in the goldfields area round Kalgoorlie and Norseman.

My experiences with growing many of these northern species in Melbourne have not been happy ones. It is such a different environment to ours; constantly in the low thirties, and with exceptionally wet summers. It is not the wet of Melbourne winters, however, but the cold which disagrees with the northern flora. This, plus often heavy, poorly-drained soils, have put paid to most of the plants I have attempted to grow. Sydney has more success, because of its warmer, drier winters, wetter summers, and (in the sandstone areas) better drainage.

There are so many interesting and unusual trees throughout this Top End, some quite flamboyant to someone more used to the rather secretive flowers of southern sclerophyll forests and heathlands, that they are rewarding for being just what they are, part of a complex environment. We discovered one of these growing along a small creek we camped beside east of Kununurra. It was a creek we found almost by accident, in a late afternoon search for a camp site. It may seem strange to say 'found almost by accident', but much of the time one drives through dry grass, often referred to as 'cane grass', more than 2.5 metres tall. It often obscures all but the tallest eucalypts, and roads are few and just narrow avenues with a wall of grass on either side. Often the only chance one has of seeing the surrounding topography is when a track takes off from the road.

It was such a track that we took on the occasion we discovered this clean, fresh stream, which contained a large number of bream-like fish. What we didn't expect to see floating in the water, though, were creamy-yellow pea flowers about 15 centimetres long. These belonged to *Sesbania formosa*, which grew to around 6 metres at the water's edge. It was the foraging of the blue-faced honeyeater, seeking nectar in these spectacular flowers, which dislodged them from the tree. 'Exotic' was the only word that seemed to suit these beautiful, almost butterfly-like blooms. At sundown the honeyeaters ceased their noisy feeding, to find roosting spots among the branches of tall pandanus palms which also grew at the edge of the creek. This, too, was a noisy procedure, as the birds settled deeply into the drier parts of the plant.

The leaves of this species, *Pandanus spiralis*, are used by the Aborigines for weaving into baskets and other useful carrying or storing equipment. The fruit of this and a number of other species is eaten in part by the Aborigines, not as a staple diet but during periods of shortage of normal food. These palms grow throughout Malaysia and in similar climates.

Leaving our little secret stream and its dark pools the next day – having breakfasted to the music of braying donkeys in the distance, and the overhead flight of two brolgas – we travelled west through extensive grassy woodlands. We crossed the wide Victoria River, entering with some suddenness rocky mesa country dotted with communities of the ever-fascinating baobabs. Each large parent tree was encircled by its youngsters, all gathered about obediently like so many children listening to stories.

At Timber Creek the Victoria River is a wide, slowly moving stretch of grey-green water. We stopped for lunch above its banks, in the sparse shade of the baobabs. Sue was unable to resist collecting the decorative fruit that lay scattered on the ground – and now hangs from our veranda rafters, ever reminding us of their northern origins, and protecting the birds from hitting our windows.

On the sun-parched slopes above the river we could hear yet more honeyeaters calling. The source of their delighted frenzy was the flowering of the small stunted *Lysiphyllum gilvum*, or 'bauhinia' whose scarlet long-tongued pea-like flowers offered welcome liquid nourishment. We were also attracted to another flowering tree, the delicate pinnate-leaved *Petalostylis labicheoides*, whose yellow-gold flowers and ferny foliage cast a light shade over the sandy ground.

Our approach to the Western Australian border was dominated by the massive jagged escarpments of the Kimberley itself, a mere handful of kilometres inside the border. The evening sun was dipping below their grand bulk, and shades of violet, purple and blue deepened as we drew nearer. Leafy-canopied *Eucalyptus bigalerita* stood scattered about the grassland, their white trunks reflecting some of the jewelled hues of the mountains. It was indeed an impressive introduction to the weeks ahead.

17 MITCHELL PLATEAU

THE KIMBERLEYS II WESTERN AUSTRALIA

Imagine waterfalls that drop level upon level, to finish in a giant basin walled in by sandstone cliffs 150 metres high; water crystal clear, never to be touched or tainted till it flows into the sea; secret caves with ancient mythological paintings few have seen; and rock shelves so warm that even on the chilliest night, with only a sleeping mat between your body and it, you lie on a warmth that radiates into you all night long.

This in a palm- and melaleuca-fringed paradise, with the barest likelihood of meeting another person, no matter how far you could walk in the one day. Almost sounds non-Australian; but this is one of our more remote wilderness areas, the Mitchell plateau in the far north-west of Western Australia.

It was the focal point of our northern trip, and the reason for our having equipped ourselves with a four-wheel-drive vehicle in Darwin. We spent a few days with friends at Kununurra while minor service and major repairs were performed on our battle-worn vehicle, a time during which we had visited Lake Argyle on the Ord River. Then we headed west on the Gibb River road, which joins the northern road to Kalumburu Mission on the far north coast.

The eastern belt of the Kimberley was the country that the Duracks had penetrated, after being dropped, in 1882, near the mouth of Cambridge Gulf, opposite what is now the site of Wyndham. They first settled on the Behn River, near its junction with the Ord River. The creation of the Ord River Scheme, and the building of Lake Argyle, meant drowning beneath its deep still waters the site of the first Durack homestead, Argyle Downs station. But the beautiful hand-built stone house was moved and now sits above the lake, its gracious architecture a monument and memorial to the determination, strength, and spirit of those pioneers. They must have driven their cattle many times over the spot where the Argyle diamond lode was later discovered.

The Pentecost River runs north into Cambridge Gulf, and this is the nearest that you approach the Timor Sea, an expanse now dotted with exploration rigs. Road conditions and river crossings ensure that you enjoy the Gibb River road at a leisurely pace. On flats where fertile soils collected, eucalypts, many of the bloodwood type, flourished; where these flats held water and formed swamps, often on the margins of creeks or rivers, one of the most spectacular species is to be found.

This is *Eucalyptus ptychocarpa* which bears masses of pink, red or occasionally white flowers, in bunches at the ends of branches. We were fortunate to locate a group in such profuse flower so early in the season, as it is generally recognised that its main flowering time is spring onwards. A sure sign that you are approaching an area where nectar is flowing from flowers is the excited calls of numerous birds drawn from afar to feed on this sweet manna. Blue-faced honeyeaters, rainbow lorikeets, shining fly-catchers and willie wagtails, combined their familiar calls as they fed on nectar or on the insects that swarmed about the blossoms. Red-tailed black cockatoos and galahs added their harsher cries to the chorus as they either wheeled in the sky above, or fed on seed on the ground or flower buds in the trees.

In the water, where there seemed to be constantly moving schools of small fish, myriad water plants, many such as *Nelumbo* and *Nymphaea*, the large-leaved water lilies that provided shelter for the water dwellers, also provided stepping pads for *Jacana*, the dainty stilt-legged waterbird commonly known as the lotus bird.

The flowers of the numerous water plants are nothing less than spectacular in their cream and variously pink shadings; and there is little growing on land to equal their flamboyance. A plant with a bunched head of flowers resembling miniature drum sticks, and with submerged hair-like leaves is, though, more unusual. This is one of the *Eriocaulon* species, which frequent slow-flowing streams and shallow ponds. This plant, possibly *E. setaceum*, is small in stature, with the dozens of erect, spreading 'drum stick' flowering stalks protruding perhaps only 5-12 centimetres out of the water. Small fish and aquatic insects use the masses of submerged fine leaves for feeding and sheltering sites. This genus, which is confined to these warmer northern waters in Australia, occurs (as *Nelumbo* the lotus lily does) throughout India, Malaysia and other similar habitats.

Because water is so concentrated in the lower areas of the north, and vegetation with any semblance of lushness is always associated with river courses or lagoons, you get a better understanding of the true nature of this country by turning your back on the wet areas and letting your gaze wander over the hills and plains beyond. At your back, a *Melaleuca leucadendron* may tower above you to more than 30 metres, its white flaky bark and soft pendulous habit reminding you of similar plants on other waterways. But your gaze is moving over grass plains, past stunted or dwarfed eucalypts, to pick up the dissected low profile plateaus that run beyond the horizon.

Spreading out their slender honey-brown branches, and covered thickly with flame-orange blossom, were communities of *Eucalyptus phoenicea*. This light, open-structured tree is a strong component of the dry ridges and rocky slopes, and the ground beneath at this time of the year is littered with discarded blooms by honeyeaters and parrots. We passed many groups of these trees, plainly at the peak of their flowering, and never failed to be impressed by the warmth of their colouring complementing so well the reds, golds and pale straw tones of the landscape.

Scattered trees or shrubs, such as the golden-flowered *Xanthostemon paradoxus*, squat in crevices where some soil has accumulated; and in the ravines where a greater depth of soil and moisture collects palms reach vertically to the open sky.

In reverse, I recall the strange sensation of having driven across these dry grass plains, through and around the often red rock forming these jump-ups, and seeing what appeared to be low dense forest ahead. It was not till we reached the edge of the plain before dropping into the Drysdale River that we realised this forest was merely the tops of *Melaleuca leucadendron* jutting out of the river above the surrounding plain.

The one constant factor of this country is the weather – and the temperature, which has little daily variation. We were to find this climate enervating in the extreme later on in our trip. In a late afternoon stop to set up camp on the Hann

River, even the local kookaburra , the blue-winged, seemed unable to raise sufficient energy to match the call of the jackass we knew. Unlike him, the blue-winged sings in pairs. When you hear them commence their song, you think that it will be the equal of Jackie's; but its range is limited and it seems to get stuck on the first few bars, tailing off to a few 'kook-kooks' as though the birds had lost their music. They are still delightful birds, and it was one of their smaller relatives, the azure kingfisher, that was to give us much pleasure late one evening on the Mitchell plateau.

Seed capsules: *Eucalyptus zygophylla*, that at left is affected by gall wasp

18 SURVEYORS POOLS

THE KIMBERLEYS III WESTERN AUSTRALIA

As you turn north from the Gibb River road onto the road which ultimately leads to the Kalumburu Mission, you immediately sense that you are leaving the main stream of traffic behind. For those who venture across the Gibb River road, skirting below the northern Kimberley, the usual direction to take at this T-junction is a southward one. Just south is Gibb River station, which used to be the refuelling point for those going north. Now, though, you need to go a further 70 kilometres south to Mt Barnett station, where fuel supplies are plentiful. The 'main stream' of traffic I mentioned previously on the Gibb River road from Kununurra amounted to four cars in two days. It is the main Great Northern Highway, the southern one from Derby to Halls Creek, which most tourists take. So by turning north, and by the time you cross the Gibb River 60 kilometres away, your sense of isolation is complete.

A number of such beautiful small rivers were to be crossed, and each had its own areas of interest, and provided an oasis of cool relief to the mostly dry hot country between. It was between two crossings in a broad claypan area that we came across a most unusual plant formation. At first glance we thought we were looking at a deserted orchard, perhaps planted by an early settler. Our common sense soon told us that this was a most unlikely place for what appeared to be apple trees.

The tree, or large apple-tree-sized shrub, was a species of *Terminalia*, possibly *T. platyphylla*, a genus represented by a number of species throughout the north. It was their grove-like formations, with little else but dry grasses around, that was so deceptive.

Wherever water held in these claypans, concentrated plant communities took advantage of the available moisture. In one small rill among sedges we found a group of *Philydrum lanuginosum*, a tall rush-like plant whose common name of frog's mouth is suggested by the shape of the open yellow flowers. I have seen this plant growing reasonably happily in a Melbourne garden, which, for a species whose natural range is across the Top End, is an indication of its hardiness.

The main river to be crossed and invariably camped on is the Drysdale, which is the main drainage line to the north for this area. It picks up the Gibb, Woodhouse, Donkey and Damper streams, on its way to becoming the eastern boundary of Kalumburu, before entering the Timor Sea at Curran Point.

As we swam in its clear cold waters washing away the dust and heat of the day's travel, with white-trunked *Melaleuca leucadendron* towering in groves on either side of the river, we wished we had carried a canoe or small boat with us to investigate downstream stretches of this winding river. We had heard that some of the country farther north, including the Carson Escarpment, contained beautiful waterfalls and gorges, and we vowed that on our next trip we would have the means of travelling on water.

Doongan station, soon after which the turn to the west to the Mitchell River homestead is taken, seemed prosperous if the kilometres of new fencing were any indication. Even though we saw few cattle and no buildings there had obviously been a large capital investment in the future grazing of this country.

It was here that we saw a new parrot (new for us) near a smooth grey rock stack we had stopped to investigate. It was multicoloured, green and blue, with yellow patches on the wings and underbody; but we unfortunately had only a 'looking up at from underneath' view. This did not enable us to determine whether it had the red rump and back of the neck which would have conclusively identified it as the mulga parrot. It was several hundred kilometres from its distribution range, according to our bird books, but there did not seem to be any other species that it could have been. Earlier, above the Gibb River, we had seen and clearly identified a male red-winged parrot, which is light green with darker green wings with a distinct red blaze and beak. (Just to illustrate that birds do not always stay inside the dotted lines on maps, a female red-winged parrot appeared at Montrose at the foothills of the Dandenongs a year before. This placed her some 400 kilometres away from her familiar areas of distribution.)

Back in warmer climates, we now reached the Mitchell River camp, on the homestead site of a former pastoral lease. It is one of two from which extensive geological exploration is undertaken. Following instructions, we took an obscure track northward, and soon began rising toward the Mitchell plateau. It was mid-afternoon, so we planned to camp that night somewhere up on the plateau. None of this time-worn landscape reaches significant elevations and much of the plateau stands at around 350 metres. Occasional taller small plateaus, which are called hills, attain nearly 500 metres.

As you leave the river flats, both the structure of the soil and the vegetation change dramatically. The rounded, lateritic profile, once common over much of the continent, and a product of long-term, water-logged soils, now forms much of this area. No longer water-logged, and free-draining, the soils here are particularly bauxite-rich. With the bauxite is associated a particular plant community, dominated by one palm in particular and to a lesser degree by two eucalypts.

In favourable soils the palms, *Livistona eatonii*, which seemed to grow no more than 6-8 metres, had their trunks so closely packed together that manoeuvring through them on horseback would have been nigh impossible. A second palm-like plant, but a cycad, grew thickly to a metre where some space was available; and *Eucalyptus miniata* and *E. tetradonta* colonised any space where *Livistona* was not too dense. *E. miniata*, which has a dark stocking base to its trunk but a clear upper trunk and branches, is spectacular when in full flower. It is long-flowering, unlike many of the trees in this high-rainfall area, which flower during the wet and disperse their seed at the onset of the dry season. The flowers of *E. miniata* are a deep orange and displayed in profusion; both parrots and the raucous nectar-feeding 'little friar bird' were making the most of the tail-end of the flowering season. *E. tetradonta* is one of the many 'bloodwoods', a group that has its maximum development in these northern monsoon zones. Like many species it carried the typical thick bark of the group, soft and not stringy, with mottled grey and yellow patches. It was not in flower, but the carpet of four-toothed (hence *tetradonta*) seed capsules covering the ground showed how profuse its flowering must be.

A coarse often tall grass up to more than 2 metres in height comprised the major ground cover, and we drove through this later on. A correct turn on the narrow two-wheeled track was often obscured by its density, and further confusion was caused by survey tracks, which were cut for aerial survey. On one occasion, as the afternoon light was fading, a wrong turn led us to a precipitous cliff edge. A second check of the map showed where the track should be, and when we reversed out it was found almost entirely obscured by the grass.

There was no need to rush through this country, anyway. By now views to the west opened up to the middle stretches of the Mitchell River and farther on to the coast about 70 kilometres away. We made camp that night on the red gravelly ground, tucked between groves of straight-trunked palms, at a point where a survey line cut a 4-metre swathe directly through the forest to the edge of the plateau. The setting sun chose the end of that pathway to display its glory, and we watched spellbound as it dipped and sank slowly into the earth, the blackness of the night and the bright stars gathering about us silently.

Up with the dawn next morning, we made for the mining camp on the Mitchell plateau from which the two main waterfall areas could be reached. Since this was private property, we had to make sure that proper courtesies were observed. We were required to inform management of both our arrival and destination, and were informed correctly and courteously that neither fuel nor assistance could be given.

We sought and were given directions to Surveyors Pools, which were on a small tributary of the Mitchell River. The track off the Port Warrender road, the proposed deep-sea port to be used for shipping bauxite, was only a few kilometres out of camp, and it proved to be steep and rough. Fire had been through, possibly the previous year, and little vegetation was growing on the black, cracked basalt soil – only weary dry grass. This unimpressive entry to the sandstone shelves above the pools hardly prepared us for the pristine beauty of the area.

As usual, our final approach was through cane grass, with the shadeless camp site being simply a clearing beside a clear small stream. Hot, and not at all impressed, we decided to follow the stream, and soon were walking over broad sandstone shelves toward more extensive walls and shelves in the near distance. Suddenly we were standing above a sharp drop and a sparkling waterfall, looking across a deep, blue pool to another waterfall cascading into it on the far side. All our doubts were dispelled. In this paradise, the more precious because we had it to ourselves, we spent delightful days exploring the succession of pools, the patches of rainforest round their edges, and the animals that abounded on the land and in the water.

The two animals that dominated the area were an amazingly agile rock wallaby, and a species of *Dasyurus*, a native spotted cat (possibly *Dasyurus hallucatus*). The small wallabies, which were not much bigger than a domestic cat, carried their fine tails back over their heads when running or standing. Their speed was lightning fast as they leapt up and across the broken sandstone shelves. They seemed to spend much of their time deep in narrow crevices or caves in the broken piles that were scattered throughout the area, coming out to feed and drink. We could flush them out of hiding simply by moving across a rock pile in which they were secreted. It was not until later that we found that this shy animal was *Peradorcas concinna*, the 'little rock wallaby'.

Dasyurus is a mammal, but is certainly not a cat. No doubt the spotted coat and long bushy tail prompted early settlers to see it as a kind of cat. Apart from one occasion when we saw a *Dasyurus* competing with a wallaby for a too-small day-time shelter, our encounters with it were at night. The antics of these small animals around the outskirts of our camp fire were nothing less than frenetic: moving quickly from one position to another, bounding, scratching, rustling, chewing, seemingly all at once. They never ventured into the area of light cast by our lamps, and usually we caught only a fleeting glimpse of them by torchlight. We did find out, though, what they were scurrying after – beetles, attracted to the firelight, and apparently a major part of their diet.

On the rock shelves above the pools, plants were generally stunted, whereas below on the water's edge *Melaleuca* and other trees grew to large proportions. While waiting patiently for wallabies to appear on one broad shelf, we sat quite still, but allowed our gaze to take in the plants around us. Within our direct vision was a dwarf gardenia less than a metre high and (tentatively identified as *G. edulis*), with a solitary highly perfumed flower; and *Calytrix exstipulata*, with masses of pink starry flowers. We had seen *Gardenia* species almost from the time we left Darwin, and though many were not traditionally attractive shrubs their white flowers were beautifully perfumed. The *Calytrix* had also been a constant companion right across the top.

White-quilled rock pigeons were in constant flight, taking off with a few noisy flaps, then gliding across the pools to alight silently on a distant shelf. They are a distinctive dark brown with a light wing patch, and we more than once spied them feeding on the fallen small figs from a *Ficus* which grew in moist soils at the base of their general habitat.

The lack of fear in otherwise shy birds was exhibited by an azure kingfisher as I sat writing beside the stream above the pools. This vivid blue and tan kookaburra-in-miniature, no more than 15 centimetres from tip to tail, was fishing for small bony bream in the late evening light. I was aware of its presence only when it left its lookout perch, inches from my head, to dart into the water. It appeared seconds later with a wriggling silver meal firmly held by its strong beak, and alighted on the same short twig, near my ear. Indications of its nearness and obvious lack of concern were the water splashes I received as the bird repeatedly whacked the fish against the perch in the familiar killing or softening-up process. He spent possibly half an hour in this position, in which time he made several more forays into the stream. He caught one more fish, and left his perch only because of pending darkness, still seeming totally unconcerned by the intruder in his favourite fishing spot.

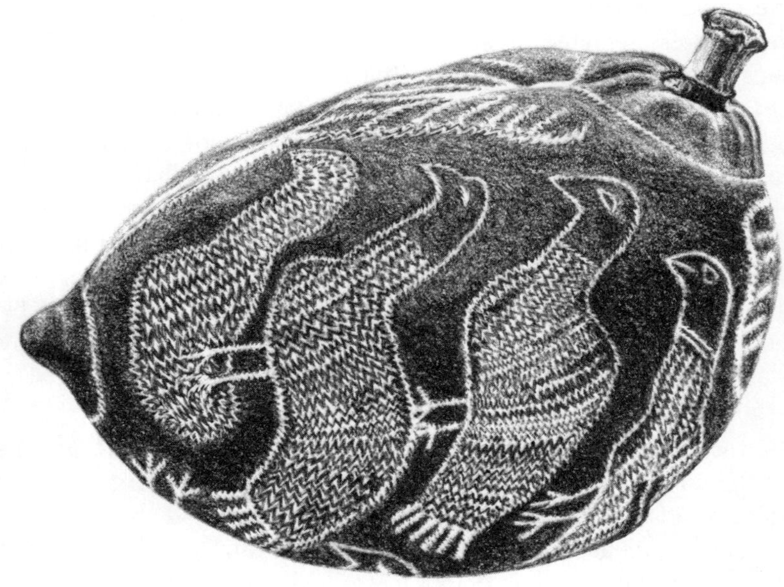

19 MITCHELL FALLS

THE KIMBERLEYS IV WESTERN AUSTRALIA

There is a time during trips such as ours to the Kimberley when you should say to yourself, 'I am not going to see anything further to match what I have just seen. Let's go home.'

Instead, nostalgically for Sue, and out of sheer greed on my part, we did look for more, down in the southern Kimberley – this after being privileged to discover, on our own, the sheer majesty and isolation of the Mitchell River Falls.

Now I'll back-track to when we finally dragged ourselves away from Surveyors Pools and drove west to Port Warrender on Admiralty Gulf. This is only a short drive from the mining camp, and before you drop the last few kilometres from the plateau to the pebbly beach an extensive view of the gulf is caught through the trunks of the Bloodwoods. You are virtually looking towards the confluence of the Indian Ocean and the Timor Sea, their collective expanse of water spreading a large barrier between you and the next main landmass.

On a rise above the beach at Port Warrender the track has been cut through a very large Aboriginal midden. I have seen many middens scattered through the dunes of coastal Victoria, but none to equal the proportions of this one. It covered an area of perhaps 300 square metres, and where the track cut through it sides of nearly a metre deep were exposed. The shells were bleached by the sun, wind, and rain, and as we drove across as well as through them we could see that they were obviously embedded to a greater depth than we could see.

We encountered more of these when we took a rough track out to Pickering Point, where we had been told we might see salt-water crocodiles sunning on the mud flats at low tide. We were too late, for the tide was coming back in quickly, and we could only imagine what lurked beneath the 'Great grey-green, greasy

Limpopo' waters swirling below us. Attacked by sandflies (midget in size, but nasty in their after-effects), we left this rather uninviting spot and made our way back to an interesting plant community we had passed on the track in.

It was a vine-thicket and situated, as they usually are, on a southern sheltered slope. I soon found, as others have, that unless you wish to rip your clothes and skin badly you walk round these patches and don't attempt to penetrate them. I could only guess at their composition, but surmised that the families Vitaceae (which contains *Cissus*) and Tiliaceae would be well represented. We heard a number of different bird calls from within the darkened thicket; but since we planned to make camp for the night within walking distance of the Mitchell Falls we had to leave their identity unsolved. We back-tracked to the mining camp and took the southern track opposite the airfield, dropping steeply through forest and then swamp, the late afternoon light rapidly fading.

The camp site was really a clearing at the end of the track, which simply peters out at a pile of broken rock among spinifex grass, *Triodia microstachya*. This grass, which covered extensive areas, even colonised outcrops of large broken rock, filling in the intervening spaces so that walking was hazardous and uncomfortable – as we found next morning on our way down to the falls. It is an enervating climate, with a consistently high temperature that some might envy; but though we were physically fit we found it necessary to strip off and immerse ourselves at regular intervals in the crystal pools we found as we pushed our way down towards the falls, following a small feeder creek. The cane grass towered above us as we broke a path through it; like the *Triodia*, it was a dry shiny straw colour. Dappled shade from the open forest provided some relief from the heat, which increased as the morning progressed.

We came suddenly to our first sight of the lower falls and the extensive basin and pool into which they drop. We had broken away from the creek that formed a smaller but still spectacular waterfall, entering the great pool on the north-eastern side through a deep narrow gorge. We had moved south-west, and suddenly found ourselves standing on the rim of a sheer-sided basin, perhaps 100 metres deep and 200 metres across.

It is easy to use adjectives like 'awe-inspiring' for effect; but such sheer, isolated beauty as this did indeed fill us with awe. As we slowly took in the grandeur of the scene, we glimpsed a little of the deep spiritual affinity that the Aborigines had developed and established with this country over thousands of years. We found a faint track leading down a dry gully to our right. It was a steep scramble for ten or fifteen minutes as we lowered our packs and ourselves carefully to the bottom, emerging eventually at the edge of the great pool we had viewed from above.

We boiled our billy amongst some rocks and, cooling our feet in the clear water, ate our lunch as we absorbed the beauty and the peace, the silence broken only by the curtain of water as it cascaded from the pools above.

Dominating the vegetation was the silver-leaved *Melaleuca argentea*, fringing the edge of the pool and actually growing in the river that flowed from it. It is a compact large shrub, and after much searching we found one out-of-season golden-yellow brush of flower. For all its apparent delicacy of foliage, we knew that it must be subjected to innundation by a raging torrent for some months. As soon as the water subsides, its buds burst open, pollination occurs, and seed is set and dispersed well before the onset of the dry season.

The depth of the pool was difficult to gauge. Though the water was clear, it was so dark that we could see only a few feet into it from the edge. Strangely, we caught sight of only one fresh-water crocodile which, being much smaller and finer in stature than its estuarine cousin, can often be mistaken from a distance for a piece of floating wood. In other places in the Kimberley these small reptiles have become used to the presence of people, but here they were extremely shy, and the one we saw quickly dropped into deeper water. They present little danger, and we felt no apprehension when swimming in the shallower water. You would not take the same licence with a salt-water crocodile. Stories of their stalking and capturing people are recorded by most writers about the north.

That night we made our camp on a broad rock platform above the water, below the sheer cliffs towering above the pool. On a warm shelf, under a clear sky, I lay for most of the night unable to sleep. I still find it difficult to discuss the feelings I had on that night: awe at being enveloped in an aura of primitive history, and even some fear because I felt an intruder. I tried to link my feelings to those of the white people who first explored this country, and to sense and absorb part of the spirituality that the Aborigines knew and lived by.

I sat and watched the vast cliffs turn from black, through grey, orange and finally sandy yellow as the dawn heralded another hot, still day. Protected by the cool shadow of the cliffs, we brewed tea and ate our breakfast, leisurely enjoying the simple comforts of our split-level rock shelf, which had given us our sleeping platform and our kitchen.

We spent the earlier, cooler part of the day investigating the plants and looking for signs of original native habitation and were rewarded in both endeavours. On shelves above possibly even the highest watermark we found clumps of an unusual small shrub with large red shiny fruits. It was *Owenia vernicosa*; and it was the size, leaf shape, and adornment of its fruits that had earned it the common name emu apple. A number of old discarded fruits, now with the shiny outer covering weathered or eaten away, lay under the shrubs. The presence of quantities of wallaby droppings in the vicinity suggested that they enjoyed the 'apples' as part of their diet. The remaining seed capsules were very hard and had a tight interlaced woven outer, which was extremely tough. I could imagine that it would take many seasons of sun and rain for moisture to penetrate to the kernel held well within this resilient container.

On a more sheltered moist shelf we found a small shrub with dainty pink flowers as big as a 50-cent piece, and with simple green leaves with yellow margins. It was an *Osbeckia*, a plant new to me, and closely related to the common garden plant *Lasiandra*, from the tropics, and *Melastoma*, from the Wallum area north of Brisbane. It was the only time that we found this pretty small shrub.

We had not yet been in a position where we could look directly at and therefore up the falls, and found that this would not be possible until we climbed the opposite side from where we entered. We were not yet ready to make this approach up and out, so we turned our attention to the north-west wall, where a patch of vegetation grew. Apart from *Hoya australis*, which typically of this genus had fleshy leaves and a scrambling habit, the plants were those we had already seen. But behind the vegetation was a shallow cave which angled down below the sheer cliff.

Its entrance was long and narrow, with boulders partly blocking our entry. Once inside there was plenty of head height – and there before us on the vertical walls was a gallery of paintings. These were mainly of animals: wallabies, native cats, crocodiles, snakes, and turtles. Many were quite faint. It was not a large gallery, and its right-hand end opened to the sky with a higher shelf above. On climbing up there we found an elongated figure painted in a horizontal pose and extending round a corner. Since we had to lean out over a drop to see the extension, we could only assume it had been painted by someone standing on another person's shoulders, or on some long-ago crumbled platform. We did not have either the experience or the techniques to ascertain how long it was since there had been Aboriginal occupation of these caves; but darker patches of sand and a sooty ceiling provided a physical and visual link with occupants of the past.

We left the cave and crossed the great pool at a narrow neck, and from there worked our way up the opposite face, climbing up a steep slope through jumbled rock and spinifex. Eventually we reached a point from where we were able to look straight at the falls, and at the wide, deep staircase created by four separate drops. Each fall was about 30 metres in width, and at this time of the year, each cascade and pool could be clearly seen, with the crystal clear water flowing in and down to the next level.

I have subsequently seen a photograph taken from a helicopter during the wet season. A tremendous torrent completely obliterated any of the individual falls. All that could be seen was a solid wall of brown water. It was hard to imagine the contrast of this other season as we cooled our hot bodies in the pool above the top fall.

As we moved northward back towards camp we found a quiet backwater of the first creek we had followed coming out. It was surrounded by *Melaleuca,* and all but covered with blue water lilies. As a backdrop there were dry outcrops on which *Eucalyptus brevifolia* was growing. A small compact, pure-white-trunked tree, it is widespread in the north. We had previously found it more often on the open plains.

From this point, we were able to see some distance to the west and south, over broken lines of sandstone, deeply etched by water and time. We thought that little of it would have been explored on foot by white men, and we wondered what could have seduced the native tribes who had lived in such close harmony with this isolated land into leaving it for the mission stations. We felt that this timeless place was waiting for the Aborigines to return to their spiritual home.

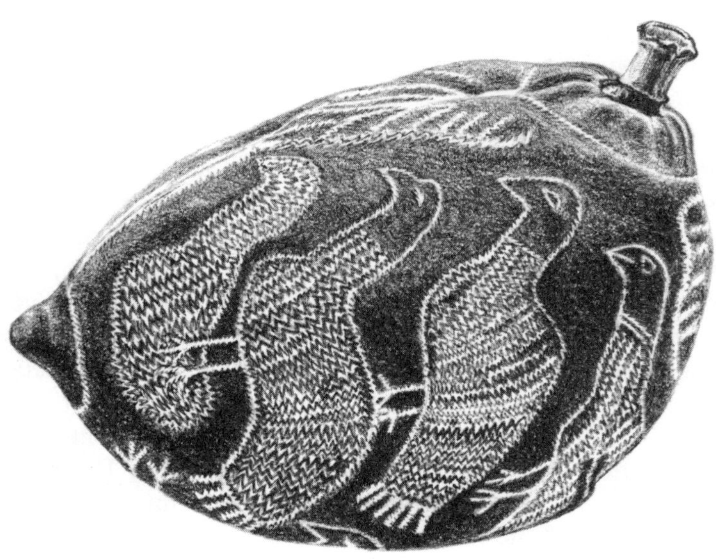

20 EPILOGUE

THE KIMBERLEYS WESTERN AUSTRALIA

From the Mitchell plateau we travelled slowly south to refuel at Barnett station. Here there seemed to be a harmonious relationship between the station owners and the Aborigines whose original tribal ground it was. The people spurned enclosed shelter in this dry time of the year, and slept beneath lean-tos of corrugated iron. The men worked on the station and the women cooked and did domestic duties around the camp and homestead.

Even though these people were not following a traditional lifestyle, the fact that they were living on their tribal lands was at least sufficient for their spiritual and emotional stability; a sharp contrast to those we saw around Fitzroy Crossing, who have been displaced from their lands.

In these intervening few days we moved farther south, and east. Gradually we left behind us the sense of wilderness we had gained and began to find indications of mass tourism. This booming industry, the product of modern affluence, gives people the opportunity to move around the country, but it does not equip them to live in harmony with it if they lack the understanding and knowledge needed to appreciate it.

At Tunnel Creek, where a decade ago you camped in isolation, you now park in line with assorted cars, buses and cross-country vehicles. The most common sight to greet you is streamers of toilet paper caught on bushes, and piles of human excreta barely off the edge of pathways. Inadequate garbage bins overflow, and their contents are scattered, with the aid of birds, for tens of metres around: cigarette packets, beer and soft drink cans, and that new environmental obscenity, the disposable nappy. This dreadful mess clearly illustrates the lack of feeling for our environment of the average tourist. There is little point in encouraging people to visit these areas if no attempt is made to educate them to understand what they are seeing and to recognise the need to protect and nurture it.

At Geikie Gorge a ranger conducting our boat trip made little attempt to enlighten his captive audience. 'They say that the cliffs are very old', he said, to explain why the river ran through ancient limestone cliffs, the obvious scene of ancient seabeds. By the halfway mark, the tourists had become more than used to yet another crocodile being pointed out sunning itself on the bank, though the trees and banks were alive with bird life requiring explanation. The few interested questioners were either ignored or answered in the briefest way; and the whole exercise was a classic one of pandering to the lowest common denominator.

The scene at Fitzroy Crossing, where the local Aborigines congregated daily at the local store, shocked us, and the memory of it will always be with us. The store is set back from the narrow dirt road, which also serves as the only entrance for tourists to Geikie Gorge and its camping area. Lining the road for some 50 metres, and extending mainly on the western side for perhaps 100 metres, was a solid sea of beer cans; solid, that is, except for gaps in which groups of Aborigines sat, emptying more cans to extend the glittering ground cover. It was indeed a sad sight, and a grave indictment of our society: for we have aided and abetted this degradation.

Wherever we saw Aborigines confined in groups to town living, they appeared to be victims of excessive alcohol. On the land, they seemed to have a greater sense of being, of contentment. In places like Fitzroy Crossing the worst obscenity is the derisive comments of people such as tourist bus operators. 'See our Abos in their natural habitat' or 'The local tinny mine, worked by the Abos'. What a dreadful impression this must have on overseas tourists!

We have a far greater responsibility to these people (and they to themselves) than is currently being exhibited. And they could, if we cared to listen, give us a greater appreciation and understanding of how to live in closer harmony with this beautiful country.

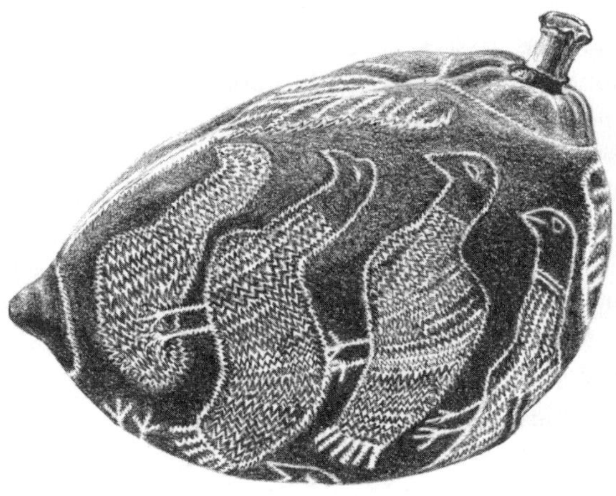

21 CARNARVON GORGE

QUEENSLAND

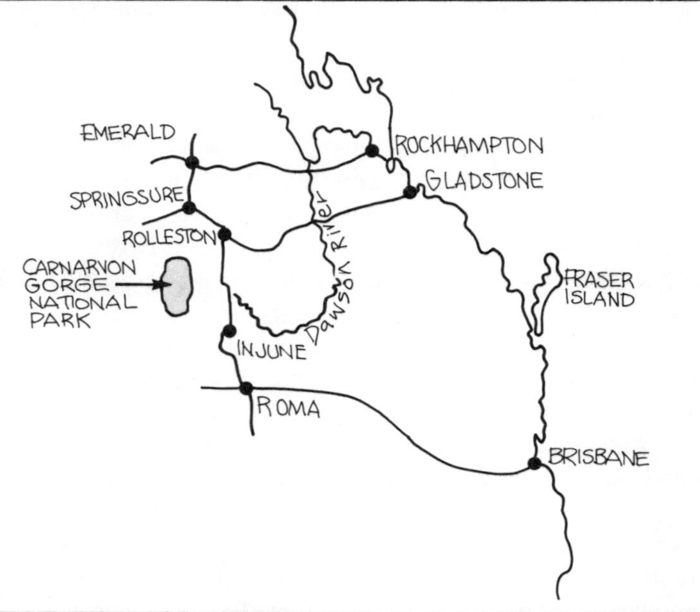

The coastal and offshore localities of Queensland are those most familiar to and favoured by tourists. The beaches, waterways and coral reefs are a mecca for sun- and pleasure-seekers. But for those seeking a different kind of fulfilment the sandstone ranges approximately 300 kilometres west of Brisbane have a different beauty and challenge.

Here the gorges of Carnarvon, Isla and Robinson cut deeply to the bedrock of these fine-grained, lightly coloured sandstones. These areas were inhabited for many thousands of years by Aboriginal tribes, which occupied specific territories either in gorges, or on the open grasslands where the gorges opened out, or on the extensive plateaus above.

Even now you can see why they chose such places as Carnarvon Gorge. Emu, kangaroo and wallaby are still plentiful; various possum species abound in the canopies of *Eucalyptus maculata* and *Eucalyptus tessellaris* that dominate the area. Fish and birds were to be had from the permanent water, and lizards and snakes from around its margins. The slowly moving, easily caught bustard or 'plains turkey' must have seemed easy game, and numerous plants offered seed and tuber.

Macrozamia, a small palm-like plant, was the source of large, red-coated and highly toxic seeds. This toxicity was removed by soaking the kernels, about the size of small onions, in the river for some days. They were then pulverised, made into a paste, and cooked over coals. This scone-like food had a high protein content and was a major source of food in late winter and spring.

Intermittent raiding occurred between the tribes – according to local knowledge this was possibly in the pursuit of young girls and boys to balance tribe numbers. These societies continued until approximately fifty years after white settlement, by which time all trace of the black inhabitants had disappeared. Records of their time there can still be seen in rock paintings and carvings, the latter of which appear to have a strong fertility significance. A gallery devoted almost entirely to vulvas of all sizes occupies a large wall in the upper gorge. Early anthropological records tell of burial holes in cliff faces; but it is likely that these would now be found only in the most remote areas.

There are many beautiful trees and plants growing both along the valley floors and on the drier tops. The one which has made the most impression horticulturally, *Grevillea longistyla*, is hardly an imposing plant in its natural habitat. I saw it first farther south at Gurrulmundi some time in the 1960s and was impressed by the large waxy pink/red flowerheads. I managed then to collect a small number of seeds from which four plants were grown. Now, some seventeen years later, the beautiful dense shrub 3 metres high with soft pinnate foliage is quite unlike the open twiggy specimens with few leaves from which my handful of seeds was collected. Growing in association is a fine-leaved form of *Banksia spinulosa* with pure golden flower spikes. This form grows to less than 2 metres, and is similar to the more compact forms found on the southern NSW coast.

Along the river banks there is *Callistemon viminalis*, whose bright red pendant brushes are a constant food source for all nectar-feeding birds. Their pendulous branches, on the ends of which the flowers hang, complement the much bolder but still weeping habit of *Casuarina cunninghamiana*, the river she-oak. This fine tree grows to large proportions along many waterways right down to southern New South Wales.

As well there are two major eucalypt species in this area. The dimpled white trunks of *Eucalyptus maculata* rise gracefully from the broad green under storey, their structural bulk and strength matching the dimensions of the towering sandstone cliffs that are so often their backdrop. The second species, *E. tessellaris*, is a beautiful, tall-shafting tree. Apart from a section of dark unusually structured bark at the base, its trunk is clear and white. It is from the formation of the bark, in squares, that the tree derives its specific name. The transition from this grey, uniform check patterning to a clear white smooth trunk is often so sudden that the bark appears to have been neatly circumcised at this point.

Once we were camped in an open-grassed area with a number of *tessellaris* growing around its perimeter, and as we were clearing up after the evening meal, on a particularly clear night, the call of a fluffy glider about to launch itself into flight sounded in a tree near by. This call is distinctive, repeated in an ever-rising pitch a number of times before the glide. For those who know this call, there may be time to grab a torch and attempt to pick up the flight path of the glider. More likely, though, the call will merely let you know that the possums are on the move, and then you can station yourself between trees to await the next flight.

These small animals have a fine membrane of skin that stretches between the wrists of the front legs and the 'ankles' of the back pair. When not stretched for gliding, the membrane folds loosely, allowing the animal normal freedom of movement over the trunks and branches of trees. Wanting to assess both the distance a glider travelled, and the line of trajectory, we waited till one landed in a tree; judged the tree to which we considered it would next move; and positioned ourselves, plus torches, in mid flight path. In a few minutes the tell-tale call of pending flight broke the quiet and we quickly shone our light toward the sound. We missed this particular take-off, not wanting to shine our torches directly into the possum's eyes, but a few seconds later it glided over our heads about 3-4 metres above the ground. Its landing, which was gentle, and with the membrane still fully extended, was made on a tree about 10-15 metres away and 2-3 metres from the base. The animal then quickly scampered up into the safety of the lower branches. This particular possum evidently had a purpose in its movements: we followed its flight from and to five trees before it settled; a total distance of about 100 metres.

In the light of day we measured an estimated height of take-off at about 5 metres, a travel distance of 14 metres, for a landing height of 3 metres. What uncanny judgment this small marsupial displayed in total darkness!

In a narrow side gorge at Carnarvon we discovered a remarkable fern which has its southern limits at about this latitude. This plant, *Angiopteris erecta*, is an oddity in that it possesses a bulbous base (rather than an elongated trunk) from which fronds spread 3-4 metres on all sides – and this from a height of about 1.5 metres. When the fronds break away from the squat base, they leave a large smooth concavity which imparts a pock-marked appearance to the surface. To my knowledge, this ancient plant is extremely rare in this part of the state. It looked much more at home on creeksides on Fraser Island, where it is a little more common. If the palms that line the main waterway of Carnarvon are an indication of a previously much wetter environment, then *Angiopteris* may just be retaining a tenuous hold in its now drier habitat.

Once out of the vicinity of the Carnarvon Gorge and to the south, the topography is flatter, with occasional low-profile sandstone jump-ups providing some relief. Cattle graze over these plains, and good camp sites free of signs of them are difficult to find. Usually we make for a flat section on higher ground, or occasionally one finds a spot in amongst *Callitris columellaris*, here called white pine to distinguish it by its silvery appearance from the darker-foliaged coastal form.

Camping amongst these trees and savouring the perfumed smoke from any offcuts you may have been fortunate to find for the fire, makes seeking out these small stands of trees all the more worthwhile. The scent of the cut wood is likened to incense, and burning simply intensifies this and spreads it on the wind.

A rare grevillea, *G. cyranostigma*, is found on top of several small outcrops at Moolyamba and Mt Playfair station in this part of the Leichardt district. This shrub, with small heads of green flowers, is closely related to *G. juniperina* which has its main area of distribution near the ACT, and northwards, sporadically to the west of Sydney, and in the Blue Mountains. The most unusual feature of *G. cyranostigma* is the elongated pollen presenter or stigma, which led Don McGillivray, a botanist friend, to inject some humour into an often dry science when he said 'The pollen presenter of this new species and the head of Cyrano de Bergerac show a particular similarity in their profiles': hence, *cyranostigma*.

Further south around Miles, there are beautiful stands of almost pure *Eucalyptus maculata*. These grow mainly on deeper soils derived from sandstone, and where shallower soils prevail, lower plant communities exist. The most outstanding shrub of this group is a member of the Rutaceae family, *Phebalium neltii*, seen to best effect in small populations. It is a pink-flowering species among a genus of predominantly yellow or cream-flowering shrubs; the pink ranges from pale to deep in shading.

Close by in an area of limited distribution is *Grevillea singuliflora* which, through its close relationship to a far distant species, again illustrates how much more widespread these plants once must have been. Both *G. singuliflora*, and *G. shiressii*, a tall shrub with eucalyptus-like leaves found growing only beside two creeks near Gosford north of Sydney, have unusual translucent blue-green flowers. These prove to be very attractive to honeyeating birds, and wattlebirds, eastern spinebills, and yellow-winged honeyeaters will all feed together in a large plant of *G. shiressii* that is in my garden. *G. singuliflora* is a miniature version of *G. shiressii* both in stature and leaf size, and though it, too, grows well in Melbourne it does so as a low, ground covering shrub.

I have wandered some distance from the towering cliffs and narrow gorges of Carnarvon, but I have done so deliberately. I wanted to illustrate the changes, sometimes abrupt, sometimes gradual, that can occur even over small distances. The interested traveller cannot help but find it a personally rewarding experience to discover how the widely differing pieces of our natural history jigsaw fit together with other discoveries from far flung corners of this vast continent.

22 TASMANIA

It is surprising how many widely travelled people have never been to Tasmania, that unique island less than an hour's flight away from Melbourne. And I wonder how many who have heard of Lake Pedder or the Franklin River as conservation issues have visited these areas?

Perhaps the singular beauties of the Apple Isle have not been publicised sufficiently. Perhaps its Government should take stock of its potential for wilderness tourism as a lucrative industry that would create an appreciation of the areas to be destroyed. Why not exploit the unusualness of Tasmania and its plants? And what an unusual flora it is! There is so much that is different in this small state, 50 per cent of which is truly wilderness, that its connections with the mainland seem remote. It was only over the land bridges which linked the two landmasses in recent times that plants common to both areas migrated – followed by the Aborigines at a much later date.

The recent acceptance of the continental drift theory answered many previously puzzling questions of plant distribution. Shared distribution with such apparently disparate countries as South America, Tasmania, and New Zealand now make more sense; and many of these shared genera have no representation on the Australian mainland.

Deciduous beech, *Nothofagus gunnii*, with foliage detail (left)

In the families Podocarpaceae, Cupressaceae, and Taxodiaceae, all of which are loosely termed 'pines', there are 10 genera which are distributed around the world. Of the family Taxodiaceae, the genus *Athrotaxis* is its only representative in the Southern Hemisphere. The three species of *Athrotaxis* occur only in Tasmania. The best known of these is *A. selaginoides*, which is greatly prized for joinery and boat-building. The handsome huon pine, *Dacrydium franklinii*, also provides valuable timber for furniture and boat construction. The popularity of these timbers led to an earlier overuse that has threatened these two large trees. There are no counterparts to these singularly beautiful and, in certain areas, dominant trees in the southern part of the mainland. We need to travel mainly to northern New South Wales or into Queensland where the large *Araucaria* or *Agathis* grow. The one exception is *Podocarpus elatus,* which can be found around Kiama in the coastal forests of south central New South Wales. Also disconcerting in Tasmania, for those used to the sclerophyll forests or heathlands of the mainland and to the familiar picture of eucalypt or acacia woodland, is the colourful sight in May or June of hillsides of autumn tonings provided by deciduous beech, *Nothofagus gunnii.* Around Waldheim Chalet in the Cradle Mountain Reserve, often just as the first heavy snowfalls start, this southern cold temperature phenomenon is seen. It is only in such areas that we see vast sheets of this golden display, beautiful yet seemingly paradoxical among the darker, more traditional landscape. The sight of the new bronzy-green beech leaves appearing in spring completes this unusual picture.

Waldheim now accommodates walkers who travel in the Cradle Mountain-Lake St Clair National Park. Apart from the chalet, which has been recently rebuilt, there are some compact, self-contained huts, with bunks and open wood stoves. With two companions I was snowed in for some days in one of these huts, and it gave us the opportunity of both observing and becoming involved with the wild life which frequents the area.

At night with a torch one doesn't actually need to venture far, before encountering either *Dasyurus maculatus,* commonly called Tiger Cat, (but it is neither a cat nor a tiger in size), or *Sarcophilus harrisii,* the Tasmanian Devil, a carnivore as big as a small dog. Both are active and adaptable scavengers and can be seen moving quickly between the huts or ferreting for morsels under logs or rocks. Torchlight is usually sufficient to frighten them away temporarily.

This was in contrast to the wallabies, ravens and possums, which could be tempted to enter the hut to accept food. They found it more difficult to search out food beneath the thick snow and, in consequence, overcame some of their fear of us in order to fill their stomachs.

In the forests and on the higher ground near Waldheim, many unusual plants are found.

Widespread elevations of alpine and subalpine areas with high rainfall have provided a continuously even environment for the evolution and development of many unusual plants. Berry-fruited shrubs have reached a high level of speciation, many noted as 'endemic to Tasmania' in botanical reference. Many of this type belong to the Epacridaceae and Ericaceae families, collectively known as heaths, and it is only now that the horticultural value of a number of these is beginning to be recognised.

Seven of the eight species of *Cyathodes,* or cheeseberries, are endemic to a range of habitats from coastal, as in *Cyathodes glauca,* to alpine, as in *Cyathodes parvifolia.* Both are medium shrubs with heath-like foliage and white flowers. A further member of the Epacrid family, *Richea,* occurs in high areas as a part of the cushion plant community. This species, *Richea minimus,* is a tight, small-foliaged cushion, with tiny white flowers sprinkled over its top. These are followed by bright red berries. The main cushion plant, *Abrotanella forsteroides,* a member of the daisy or Asteraceae family, forms extensive and often co-existent communities with a second daisy, *Pterygopappus lawrencei*. Neither has significant flowers, and it is their rock-hard mounds of bright green (which look invitingly soft) for which they are really known. In alpine areas of New Zealand, plants of this extraordinary appearance are called vegetable sheep, an allusion to the shape of a heavily woolled sheep at rest.

If assessment of fossils is accurate, the animal population of Tasmania has altered considerably in the past 10 000–20 000 years. In this time two types of kangaroo have become extinct. It has been suggested that the encroachment of forest into their browsing lands reduced food below a level sufficient to maintain viable populations. Doubtless plant populations also suffered, with some being irrevocably affected. Others which have survived have done so by adaptation.

At some stage in its evolutionary history, *Prionotes cerinthoides*, a spectacular climbing epacrid, took to the trees. In the moist gully areas it is indeed a sight to behold as it festoons mossy trunks and branches with its red waxy bells. It takes advantage of space not occupied by competitive plants and climbs its way high into the branches of tall trees. It is not widely grown or known in horticulture, but if you are fortunate enough to obtain a plant, a simulation of natural growing conditions will give slow but satisfactory results. A terracotta pot filled with a mix of fern pieces and sphagnum moss, or a living fern trunk into which a rooted cutting can be inserted, are two methods which can be used successfully. Shade and moisture are essential.

Also with a red bell flower, but unrelated, is *Blandfordia punicea*, the Christmas Bell of Tasmania. This is very similar in appearance to those found in New South Wales and Queensland, but it is often found in harsher, colder environments than either *Blandfordia nobilis* or *Blandfordia grandiflora*. All are difficult to detect when not in flower, since their thin rush-like foliage blends in with sedges and grasses; but the large pendant flowers soon attract attention when they open. Though *Blandfordia* takes a number of years to flower, its summer beauty is worth the wait. Here, too, is an instance of disjunct distribution of a genus; for even though Victoria has many habitats suitable for Christmas Bells they do not occur in this state.

Among the diverse epacrids of Tasmania the largest members are *Richea scoparia*, *R. dracophylla* and *R. pandanifolia*. They are erect shrubs whose rigid tapering leaves are reminiscent of a pineapple plant, and in sheltered areas the first two species can grow up to 3-5 metres; the third can grow to 12 metres. The first has flowerheads of pink or red. The second can spread to a metre across, and has cream inflorescences. The third, *R. pandanifolia*, named for its similarity to a pandanus palm, has a leaf span of well over a metre, with much of this atop a tall bare trunk. Flower colour varies from white to deep pink.

Lomatia, a member of the Proteaceae family, is represented in Australia by about ten species, three in Tasmania. All those known were cream-flowered, until recently, when *Lomatia tasmanica* was discovered in the far south-west of Tasmania, near Port Davey. This tall species, with pinnate leaves, is the only representative with red flowers. *Lomatia tinctoria,* from drier forest areas, is a small shrub with finely divided foliage and sprays of cream flowers.

The niches so often filled on the mainland by species of *Grevillea* are often occupied in Tasmania by other members of the Proteaceae family. We have few if any representatives of these southern groups on the mainland. *Agastachys,* the white waratah, and *Cenarrenes,* the native plum, are two that occur only in Tasmania and have only one species each.

Agastachys odorata can be a medium tree in shaded moist sites, with long thick tapering leaves. The highly perfumed flowers from which the specific name derives are cream, and held above the foliage in an erect spike. *Cenarrenes nitida* is also a medium-sized tree with thickish leaves, but with some irregularity along the margins. The cream flowers are followed by a black succulent fruit which gives rise to the common name.

The western and south-western parts of Tasmania experience higher rainfall than the eastern sector because of the general elevation of the land. This has been the major force in carving deep into the mainly quartzite rock the breathtaking gorges and rivers for which the area is world famous.

This spectacularly beautiful topography has reached its present shape only through a long complicated process. To look at this irregularly folded, twisted, dipping rock, seen as jagged white teeth at high elevations, or smooth, orange and marble-like where the waters of the Franklin and Gordon Rivers have eroded and polished it for millions of years, is to see land-form without counterpart on the mainland.

These ranges were once basins of sedimentary rock which had extreme pressures applied to them by massive tectonic forces. These were of such magnitude as to alter the rock into a different kind: quartzite. Since then, this rock has been eroded, then covered by seas, and later again uplifted by further vast tectonic force for the processes of erosion by wind, rain and sun to begin all over again.

Because of the rugged terrain, the construction of roads into most of this area is not practical. While those who do not care to stir from the roads can gain some appreciation from afar, it is mainly country for hardy bush walkers, who gain the rewards of their efforts in the beauty and tranquility they find. The canoeist, too, on such expeditions as the Franklin River trip, which ends at Macquarie Harbour, where the town of Strahan is situated, is another who is able to experience the breathtaking isolation of this ancient wilderness.

One area which does provide some opportunity of close involvement with the rugged landscape is the new Lake Pedder, Lake Gordon area. Even though this area is in the western half of the state, it has to be approached from the east, either from Hobart or the Lakes Highway which comes in from the north-west and joins the road from Hobart.

I was one of the fortunates who walked into the real Lake Pedder to pay our last tributes to a pristine area, before it was substantially enlarged as a reservoir for future hydro-electricity production. People driving there now and viewing the long, sharp-fronted Franklin Range reflected in the water on a still day, or the dramatic colour change of the rock and water at sunset, may wonder how it could be any more beautiful than it is now. But it was. Where the southern waters of the lake now lap against the man-made wall of Scott's Peak dam, was the beginning of a 15-kilometre walk to Lake Pedder over button-grass plains. These were regularly cut by deep, narrow creeks, which were invariably tea-coloured from the mostly less than knee high vegetation. Always in sight were the jagged peaks of the ranges which flanked Lake Pedder; and to the north was a now submerged tributary of the Anne River, much wider and deeper than any of the smaller creeks on the plains, its banks lined with taller vegetation.

It was not until one breasted a sand ridge, which was the lake's eastern limit, that the full beauty of the lake and the broad white beach running for a kilometre or more came into view and the total panorama of the area could be absorbed. It was this sharply faced dune, or lunette, formed by westerly winds from sands blown from the exposed shore platform, that held back the waters of Lake Pedder. The waters of Maria Creek, fed by Lake Maria, cut around the northern end of the lunette as the main lake's constant source. In the north-west corner, the lake overflowed to become the Serpentine River, which wound its snake-like path across the plains and around the ranges before it submitted to the larger mass of the Gordon River. This ancient system, formed by a combination of wind, snow, water and ice, was unique. It is now underwater forever, and its full scientific individuality will never be gauged.

After leaving Lake Pedder, and moving east, you gradually enter forests which become taller where soil change and depth allows. If you continue to drive through these stands of *Eucalyptus delegatensis* without stopping to investigate gullies or slopes beside the road, you will miss an experience. Here, just off the bitumen or gravel in the deeper cooler environment shaded by the interlocking canopy of the trees, is a fairy world. Everything in sight appears to be festooned with moss, like light green cobwebs. This effect is highlighted by red or purple fringes of lichen growing on fallen trunks or protruding through the dense leaf litter like so many bright lanterns.

The rainfall in the western ranges and central plateau is higher than in the east, and it is not uncommon to encounter these mysterious lower forest environments in the plateau region. *E. delegatensis* is one of a number of eucalypt species shared with the mainland. But intervals of isolation in Tasmania's history have been of such length that a number of endemic species have evolved in varying localities in the state. In fact, of a probable list of twenty-nine species, fifteen are found only in Tasmania. Whereas on the mainland only *Eucalyptus pauciflora* is found above the snowline, this one and two others occur here in Tasmania.

One, *E. vernicosa*, occurs on such snow-covered areas as Cradle Mountain or at Hartz Mountain in the south-east. At best it is a large shrub, but often it grows no higher than 60 centimetres. The varnished leaves from which the specific name is derived are very small for the genus, being only a centimetre long and the same width in extreme cases. A leaf measuring 5 centimetres is large for the species.

The other, *E. coccifera*, is commonly called Tasmanian Snow Gum and it is widespread over much of the state to an altitude of around 1400 metres. This attractive small tree with compound flower heads is grown widely outside its state of origin and it has adapted well to environments hotter and drier than those from which it originates.

Found well below the snowline and extending to sea level is one of the bigger endemic eucalypts: *E. cordata*, which can grow to 30 metres high. Older trees in cultivation are mostly about 10 metres, however, and it is a striking, shapely tree, which carries its rounded, grey, juvenile leaves into adulthood.

Two plants of the rainforests and creeksides are so unusual as to warrant special mention. Both are common in these habitats and the first, *Anodopetalum biglandulosum*, has a most unusual growing habit. Once the slender trunk attains a certain height, depending on the particular environment in which it is growing, it bends over horizontal to the ground. The branches grow up and then they, too, grow horizontally. The overall effect where there are almost pure stands of 'horizontal' (as it is locally known), is an often impenetrable platform metres thick. Many a bush walker has had to make their way around these singularly unusual communities.

The second plant, *Eucryphia lucida*, is well known for being a prolific source of honey, sold world-wide as 'Leatherwood Honey'. *Eucryphia lucida* can form a tree in the most sheltered sites, or a large shrub where the situation is more exposed. It has coarse leaves up to 4 centimetres long, and the quite large flowers are a delicate pink or white. In hotter, drier climates it can be grown successfully where some shade and moisture are available.

The smaller *Eucryphia milliganii* is less well known, but some of the honey supplied by *E. lucida* is probably contributed by this species. They are known to hybridise, a fact which makes identification difficult. A third species, *E. moorei*, occurs in sheltered, near-coastal jungles of eastern Victorian and southern New South Wales. I have seen it in deep gullies on the Howe Range, where it is a tall straight-trunked tree with softer, more pinnate leaves than either of the Tasmanian species.

There is no doubt that it is the central and western parts of Tasmania which offer the greatest opportunities for 'getting away from civilisation'. The vast ranges of wild mountains, deep beautiful gorges, and enchanting forests are all worth seeking out and enjoying; in these remote areas there is always the possibility that you may be the lucky person who has the good fortune to see *Thylacinus*, the elusive Tasmanian Tiger. This dog-like marsupial, with a striped body and long tapering tail, was once numerous in Tasmania, but has been seen only fleetingly over the past fifty or more years. Some scientists believe its numbers are increasing, and if it is definitely proved to be still extant, it will be a tribute to the persistence of those who have never given up hope of its survival as a species.

23 NADGEE FAUNAL RESERVE

NEW SOUTH WALES

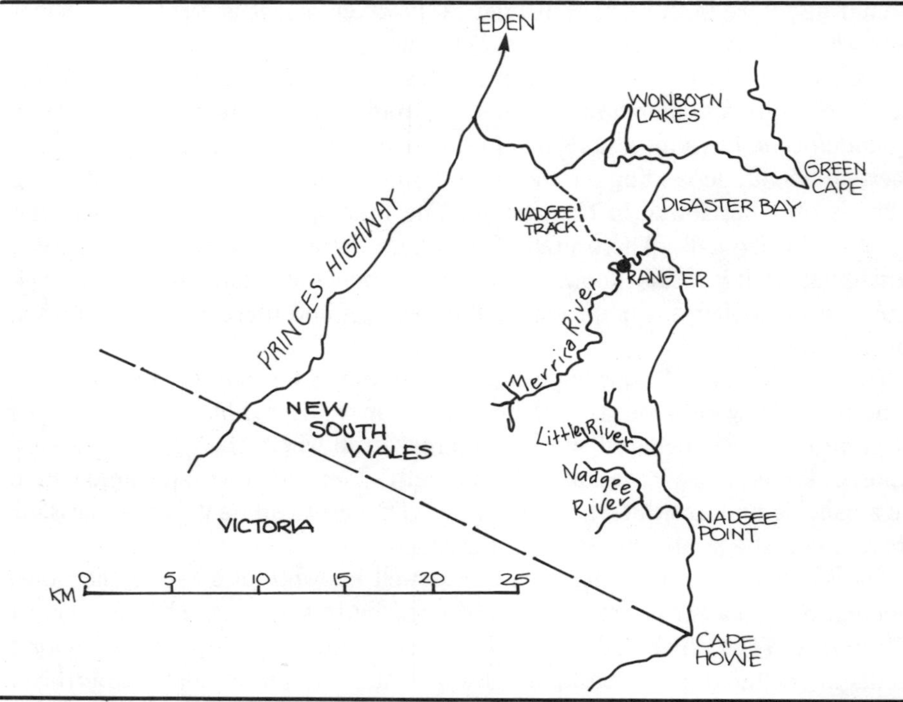

Abutting the Howe Range on the New South Wales side of the Victorian border is the Nadgee Nature Reserve. Authorities showed vision when they set aside this diverse area, which rises from behind nearly 40 kilometres of coastline. The Reserve is now set aside solely for scientific research, but in its earlier days limited numbers of people were allowed in to camp.

The only approach is a branch track from the Wonboyn Lakes road, with a final fording of the Merrica River, which is the northern boundary of the Reserve. This broad but generally shallow river rises and falls within the Reserve and, as happened to me, can imprison you if heavy rains flood the river within a few hours. Its mouth is at the eastern boundary; and runs between steep cliffs festooned with *Dendrobium speciosum*, a rock-dwelling orchid with large leaves, and massed sprays of cream flowers. Some have fallen with loose rocks from their cliff holds, and perch atop large boulders at the water's edge.

Few 'wattles' equal the fine, weeping *Acacia cognata* (top). Often found near streams in southern New South Wales and eastern Victoria, its soft skirt sweeps the ground, forming an effective windbreak. This contrasts with *Eucalyptus salubris* (below). This sensuous, shining copper-coloured tree is a dominant component of the landscape near Norseman, WA.

Overleaf: three very different and beautiful plants found at Dongara. *Billardiera ringens* (left) used basically as a climbing, screening plant in cultivation, forms dense mounds on the limestone south of Dongara. Opposite it nature's beautiful landscape example – subtly different pinks in a group of *Pimelea ferruginea* – is one we could extract and use in our own gardens. Below: few plants of the sand-plain or Kwongan have the soft textures of the northern *Xanthosia tomentosa,* a grey, felt-leaved low-growing plant, with pink-flushed, cream flowers

Our winter-flooded water area, which reaches almost to our front steps, now holds many populations of breeding water birds; just four years ago it was a bare cow paddock

The large colonies of oysters indicated that few people ventured here even before the area was reserved. No doubt many were deterred by the 7-kilometre walk or the tricky boat ride. The magnificent sea eagles are perfectly at home here, with great expanses of sea in which to fish, and a quiet estuary with tall forests in which to build their nests. They are different in colour to the wedgetail eagle, being mostly white beneath with grey wings, and with a call more like that of a goose. Coming from high in a hidden perching spot, its honking call can be disconcerting until you get used to it. Juvenile birds are mottled brown, and have been confused with wedgetails, but do not possess the distinctive tail shape that gives this more common bird its popular name.

Two creatures are plentiful throughout this area – black snakes and ticks. The snakes frequent grassland, forest, and coastal headland, and love to sun themselves on just about every rock shelf in the creeks and rivers. I have found them generally very shy, and on my numerous encounters with them they quickly withdrew to safety. But on one occasion I came across a large black snake so totally engrossed in what he was doing that he was oblivious of my presence. He was lying full length in a shallow grass-bottomed pool, which was packed with tadpoles; and, as you can imagine, gorging himself on this easy meal.

The ticks are often in the large *Acacia cognatas* that line the creeks, and fall on you as you brush against the fine, scented foliage. They usually attach themselves to the base of the hairline at the back of the neck, the armpits, or the crotch and, if not detected, can pump sufficient toxin into you to produce a fever condition of varying intensity. A nightly tick hunt by torchlight was a necessary precaution, and any that were found were dotted with turpentine until they released their hold. Attempting to pull them out generally leaves the head firmly embedded, and this of course, allows the infection to continue. It is interesting to note that here, and in other tick zones such as Mallacoota, the local fauna have a natural resistance to ticks.

The coastal heathlands, which can be followed for around 15 kilometres, contain interesting flora, and are cut by delightful inlets and short rivers. The rise and fall of these numerous streams have an even shorter life from the Table Hills range than the Merrica River. As you walk westward about 30 metres above sea level, the sharp escarpment of the range is in constant view to your right. In the mid 1960s I had volunteered to start a herbarium for the then ranger, David Hope, and had received permission to collect specimens which I would later identify, press and mount.

Many that were collected were those you would expect to find in such heathlands: *Epacris impressa, Correa reflexa, Leptospermum myrsinoides, Acacia suaveolens,* which are typical components of many such areas. The surprises were *Boronia pinnata* in moist depressions; along with *Howittia trilocularis,* with felted leaves and purple flowers; and *Phebalium squamulosum* var. *argenteum*, a small windblown silvery bush growing in shallow gullies, open to the full blast of the wind. This and another plant, *Spyridium parvifolium* – which I also found on the Howe Range heathlands, and which is totally prostrate in both sites – are usually taller forest plants in moister situations. The constant wind, salt-laden and strong, ensures that these coastal plants remain compact in stature.

From these windswept areas a considerable drop is made to the inlet formed by the confluence of the north and south arms of Little River. It is surprisingly large and fringed with forests, mainly *Eucalyptus globulus* ssp. *pseudo-globulus*, tall, white-trunked and long-leaved; and *E. botryoides*, with dark barked base and clean upper trunk and branches, which can be cream to salmon-coloured. Both reach large proportions in this ideal environment; but the nearer they approach the beach and the wind influences the more reduced in stature they become.

The headland on the western side of the inlet was the last place where I was able to find *Banksia paludosa*, whose distribution I had been plotting. This common NSW shrub, with yellow brushes and stiff foliage, was believed to also occur in Victoria; but I think that this point is about the limit of its westward migration.

Hakea macreana, a beautiful large shrub with soft needle leaves and sprays of white flowers, also has its southern limits within Nadgee's boundaries. It is a relatively common plant of the tablelands, and is pine- or casuarina-like in appearance, with a weeping habit.

Just below the heathland on which *Banksia paludosa* grows, *Grevillea lanigera* can be found among spinifex and *Correa alba*. This woolly-leaved shrub with cream or pink flowers does not have a wide distribution, but within this it grows from shoreline to subalpine sites. Here, as at Wilsons Promontory, it is a low wind-blown mound, whereas on stream-sides in the forests of eastern Gippsland it can attain nearly 2 metres.

It always pleases me, no matter how much country I travel and how many plants I see, to find one in an unexpected habitat. The plant was *Eucalyptus sideroxylon*, the 'red ironbark'; the place was the slopes above Jane Spier's Beach. This remote area is in the northern sector of the Reserve, and is reached by a pleasant walking track from the Table Hills. It is the lower access track for firefighting, and terminates at the Merrica River mouth. The eucalypts, tall and straight trunked, with black deeply furrowed bark, dominate the southerly slopes before the final drop to the beach.

The main areas of distribution for this beautiful tree, which often has pink flowers, is mostly amongst box or white ironbark forest in central Victoria, or on drier rocky hillsides on the tablelands. To look down, then, through regimented black trunks to the gently moving southern Pacific Ocean, was, for me, unusual and disorientating. Once on the beach you can look back up to the slope and clearly distinguish the dark trunks with their familiar grey-leaved canopies.

There is a great sense of isolation on this coastline, and the broad sandy beach encourages you to walk on and investigate the next distant headland. We had reached the beach early in the morning and not long after high tide, to find only a few seagulls in possession of miles of sand.

Obviously, though, there had been an earlier visitor. Canine footprints were clearly those of a dingo on an early morning food search. This solitary forager had left an unmistakable signature. While he left clear footprints with both his near paws and offside front paw, only a hole in the sand represented his rear offside leg. He must have fallen victim to a trap, and had either dragged his paw off or had bitten it off to free himself from this vicious impediment. He left a distinctive trail of intent as he walked the whole length of the beach; moving from the shoreline to investigate a pile of kelp, then back to a pile of rocks high on the beach, before returning again to where the gentle waves left some new flotsam on the sand as they receded. No doubt this brave warrior journeyed the beach often; and it was comforting to know that he could forage safely within the boundaries of the sanctuary of Nadgee.

As we walked back toward the tableland, engrossed in our individual fantasies about the peg-leg dingo, the first flock of red-tailed black cockatoos I had ever sighted drifted overhead. They are large birds of vividly contrasting colours, the black of a shining metallic intensity, and the red a brilliant splash of colour across the jet black feathers. Their territory is normally farther north, but a number of recordings for this part of the coast have been made.

Fire has devastated the area twice within the time I have known it. Logging occurs to the banks of the waterways within it. Somehow, though, it survives and regenerates, to delight and inform those who wish to learn from its vast storehouse of natural history.

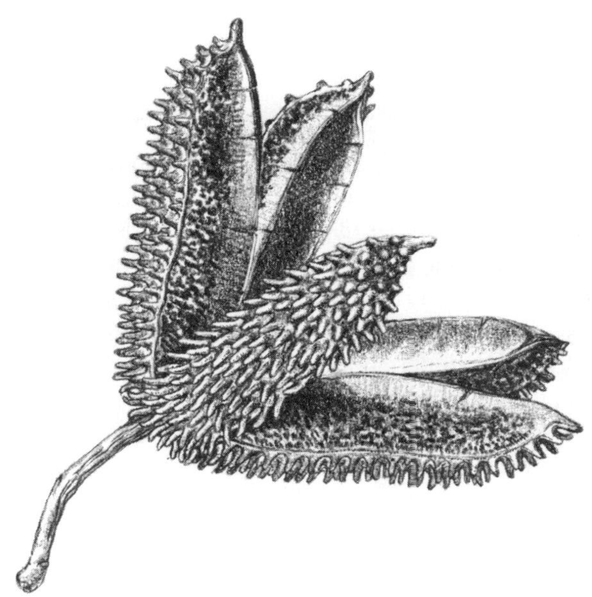

Flindersia maculata

24 KANGAROO ISLAND

SOUTH AUSTRALIA

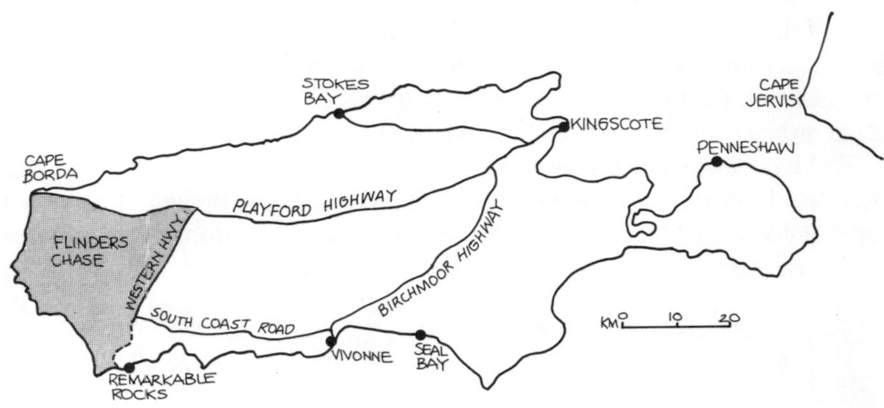

Kangaroo Island, a relatively small annexe of South Australia, lies only 20-odd kilometres off the Fleurieu Peninsula and represents both the eastern and western limits of a number of plant species. It also has a considerable number of endemic species; that is, plants which occur only on the island.

The island is less than 150 kilometres in length, and much of the central and eastern areas are occupied by farms and towns. The western end, where the Flinders Chase National Park is situated, is quite different with denser areas of vegetation and windswept headlands. The dominant landforms are of limestone and granite. The former is mostly of a low stature (as is most of the island) and Mt Taylor, in the mid-western area, is given this inflated title only because of its minimal projection above flat mallee country. The granite, though, has beautifully sculptured forms at Remarkable Rocks on the south coast.

Here the elements have carved into the less resistant sections of large isolated tors – a slow process that has produced these large fluted, domed and hollowed free-form sculptures, silhouetted against the sky and ocean. To the west of these is an extensive area of cliff limestone overlying granite; and colonising the shallow calcareous soils that have formed from this is a dwarf form of *Banksia ornata*. This plant, which has toothed grey-green foliage and orange-yellow flower heads,

Remarkable Rocks

is a familiar component of the sand-dune structure of the Big and Little Deserts in Victoria and in South Australia, and is often a large spreading shrub. Here the form of this population was very compact: a response to the windswept and low-moisture environment.

Still on the limestone, but farther away from the direct force of the wind, we found *Correa decumbens* near a small population of *Eucalyptus baxteri* growing in gravelly soil. Its familiar dark brown interwoven bark places *E. baxteri* in the stringybark group, and it can be a very large tree. But the environment here, as often happens in Victoria in similar sites, reduces its growth to no more than 2.5 metres. The *Correa* is low and spreading and differs from other *Correa* species in having its red and green tubular flowers upturned.

Kangaroo Island is the western limit for both these species, as it is for *Epacris impressa*, which grew on adjacent heathlands. This common component of eastern heath and woodland, like the other plants mentioned, has had its western progress halted by the arid barriers of desert – the major barrier, of course, being the Nullarbor Plain.

Three members of the Proteaceae family that are wide-ranging in south-western Australian sandplain and laterite soils have their eastern outliers either on Kangaroo Island or on the mainland close by. *Adenanthos sericea*, which has soft grey finely divided leaves and small yellow or red tubular flowers, forms sparse communities on deeper soils. Often it grows on road verges where its hold is tenuous. Also, bordering farmland, we found a limited stand of *Hakea*, which we assumed to be either *Hakea multilineata* or *Hakea francisiana*. As with the *Adenanthos*, it was a shock to find this plant so far from its main area of occurrence and, in this instance, growing as a barely surviving small population of six plants. I recognised it by its foliage, for it was neither in flower nor bearing seed.

The third 'westerner' was *Grevillea pauciflora*, a small shrub with grey leaves, and red flowers that are never prolific. Though we saw only a few small groups of this plant here, one can follow it for hundreds of kilometres across the southern sand and mallee heathlands of Western Australia.

These are not the only plants now locked into these habitats by dramatic climatic and topographical changes. A whole group of mallee eucalypts can be found on either side of the Nullarbor; and, apart from small areas where no trees grow at all, some species can be found growing on both sides of the treeless zone. *Eucalyptus diversifolia* is one such plant. I have seen it growing near the Portland lighthouse in Victoria; as a dwarfed shrub on Kangaroo Island; no more than 15 centimetres high on the edge of the Great Australian Bight cliffs; and finally as a large-fruited mallee a few kilometres east of Norseman, south of Kalgoorlie in Western Australia. Overall, this covers a distance of approximately 2600 kilometres. Think of the length of time that the aridity of the Nullarbor has presented a barrier to tree movement and you will appreciate the ancient nature of eucalypts.

Two other eucalypts, *E. cneorifolia*, which has its main distribution on Kangaroo Island, and *E. remota*, a mallee ash related to the eastern *E. sieberi* and found only about Mt Taylor, can be added to the check list of the island's plants. The first is a dense shrub or small tree, with a compact crown of very fine leaves. Fortunately, some agriculturalist realised the potential of this tree for shelter belts and windbreaks. This meant that many were left in large groups, and now they or their progeny add a beautiful aspect to the undulating grazing land in the centre of the island.

On the other pastured lands, two more plants, *Xanthorrhoea tateana* (grass tree) and *Eucalyptus cosmophylla* (cup gum), remind us of the ancient character of the natural landscape.

The grass tree is of massive proportions, some ancient specimens reaching nearly 4 metres in height. With a flower spike of similar proportions, and a pendulous skirt of grassy foliage atop the oft-burnt trunk, these grand specimens, often growing in colonies, present an imposing sight.

Eucalyptus cosmophylla grows over much of the island and the adjacent mainland, but is seen to best advantage on the margins of rural land. It is only small in stature, with a lightly barked lower trunk, and broad, grey-green leaves. The buds are large, and when in flower the tree provides a good nectar source in late autumn and in winter. The flower colour is creamy-white, and the blossoms are borne in profusion, almost as though a giant bottle of cream were poured over the canopy. These are beautiful trees, not only in their flowering but in their habit and form and the way in which they present themselves as part of a population rather than as a lone specimen (with variation of leaf colour, or bud and flower texture).

The seal populations east of Vivonne Bay on the south coast are a further aspect of the island's natural history. And the lighthouse of Cape Borda on the northern boundary of Flinders Chase National Park is one of the man-made structures worth inspecting.

Flinders Chase, where Cape Barren geese can be seen in a controlled range situation, is moister than the eastern end of the island. As a consequence, plant populations are more recognisable to someone from similar parts of Victoria.

If you take your own vehicle across to the island you can easily find any number of secluded caves and beaches and escape the crowds that congregate at Kingscote and American River.

Eucalyptus coronata

25 LABERTOUCHE

VICTORIA

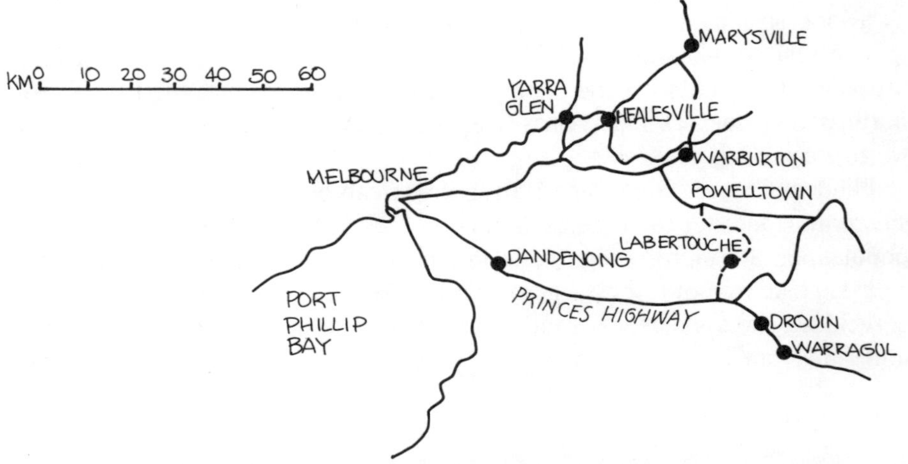

The ancient nature of many plants is clearly illustrated by both the distances which separate populations and the physical changes exhibited by them.

Less than an hour from my home three of Victoria's rare plants occur. One of these, *Grevillea barklyana*, is by far the biggest member of this genus in Victoria. It grows in the deep gullies of the headwaters of the Bunyip and Tarago rivers at Labertouche. If you drove only along the Princes Highway between Drouin and Pakenham, or on the Noojee/Yarra Junction road on the top of the range, you would never see it. Yet in the gullies it grows in profusion, apparently happy with its roots often in water, and often attaining more than 8-10 metres in height. It has large, irregularly lobed leaves, reminiscent of many northern Australian rainforest trees, and pink 'toothbrush' flowering spikes.

Even as the crow flies, it is a 600-kilometre journey past and over the Great Divide, and numerous other ranges, before you find the plant again at Ulladulla on the south central NSW coast. Here it is a compact large shrub, with mostly entire leaves, growing on coastal heathlands in the full blast of the ocean winds. The few plants that survive in this habitat are under threat from housing development, which is spreading inexorably toward the cliff edge of the heathlands.

The plant associations of *Grevillea barklyana* in these disparate habitats are, as can well be imagined, very different. At Ulladulla the species are fairly typical of coastal heathlands vegetation in this region. Strong components are dwarfed *Eucalyptus obliqua, Kunzea ambigua*, with its sweetly perfumed fluffy white flowers, and *Melaleuca hypericifolia*, its stature altering from a small shrub to a ground-hugging plant the more exposed it becomes to winds. *Epacris, Leptospermum, Banksia, Isopogon* and *Conospermum*, are among the genera that a person familiar with heathland flora expects to encounter, and does.

On my first visit to Ulladulla, I found a plant that took a lot of head scratching and book searching to identify. It turned out to be a dwarf member of the native pine family, *Podocarpus spinulosus*. Unlike *P. elatus*, the tall tree of moister localities, which I knew reasonably well, and the small-leaved *P. lawrencei*, the tough rock-hugging plant of alpine areas, this species was growing as a small stunted shrub in a harsh, dry environment.

Back to the south-west, across the Snowy Mountains and the high country of Gippsland, the Victorian *Grevillea barklyana* is surrounded by plants that thrive in a heavy red soil, with much higher rainfall and little exposure to wind.

From the flat area around Labertouche, you quickly climb and wind up into fern gullies where you find towering *Eucalyptus viminalis*, with long streamers of peeled bark hanging from the white trunks and branches. *Bedfordia salicina* and *Olearia argophylla*, both large shrubs with big pendulous leaves, crowd together above the ferns and line most gullies. Where space is available, either *Prostanthera lasianthos*, which flowers around Christmas time, or *P. melissifolia*, whose blue or pink flowers bloom earlier, take their opportunity to form colonies.

Left to right: *Grevillea barklyana* *Boronia muelleri* *Astelia nervosa*

On higher, drier slopes, *Pultenaea juniperina*, yellow-flowered and densely suckering in habit, forms thickets around 2 metres tall. It is while climbing up these winding tracks, with the constant expectation of a lyrebird crossing the road in panicky flight, that you see the second rare plant of this area flowering in spring. This is *Boronia muelleri*, again a plant with a disjointed distribution, which can grow to very large proportions. Mostly it is found in shaded, moist environments, including the Otway Ranges in western Victoria and suitable areas of far East Gippsland and southern NSW. It is recorded as attaining a height of 10 metres, an unusual size for this genus – and what a magnificent sight a plant of this height must be in full bloom!

Like many boronias, this one has fine pinnate foliage and masses of white to deep pink flowers, the whole plant suffused with a delicate fragrance. Shrubs of 3-4 metres in height are not unusual at Labertouche, but most plants would be around 2 metres. At Wingan Inlet, in east Gippsland, *Boronia muelleri* is also generally of this stature, though it is in a drier environment and grows in a soil with a lower humus level. I have cultivated plants from both areas, and found little difference in their ability to adapt to garden conditions.

The higher you drive into the range above Labertouche, the drier the environment becomes, and you come across extensive areas of exposed granite. *Callistemon pallidus*, the lemon bottlebrush, is a dominant component of these outcrops, and grows and flowers even where little soil seems to exist. It occupies a number of outcrops of these eastern highlands – Ben Cairn, above Warburton, Cumberland Falls near Marysville, and virtually at my back door on Mt St Leonard. At Wilsons Promontory it is found atop Mt Oberon, where the strong southerlies have pruned it to a compact shape. It also found its way to Tasmania, no doubt by way of an ancient land bridge, and there it occupies similar drier localities. In east Gippsland, on such streams as Freestone and Valencia creeks, it is taller and wispier, and the brushes are smaller and paler in colour than is usual. A deep pink-flowered plant which is attributed to *C. pallidus*, grows on a rocky island in the Avon River, with the creamy-yellow form growing along the banks.

As we sat on a rock gazing back down into the basin which was the catchment area for the Bunyip and Tarago rivers, two sounds, one pleasant, the other totally invasive, were constantly with us. The first was the quiet calling of feeding honeyeaters, with an occasional raucous blast from a wattle bird; the second the scream of trail bikes, whose riders defied barriers, logs, and rock shelves to ride to the top of the rocks.

After returning to our car we drove east along an old timber track to the head of a gully running down the north side of the range. We had been told that in this area, growing in very wet pockets, we might find *Astelia nervosa*, a tall lily found only in a few such areas in this locality. The path in to the patch we were seeking was flanked by large *Nothofagus cunninghamii*, the forest beech, found throughout these moist highlands.

Acacia melanoxylon, blackwoods, were also here, growing to large tree proportions; but even these were dwarfed by *Eucalyptus regnans*, the mountain ash recognised as the tallest hardwood in the world. The low, tangled vegetation was dominated by *Bauera rubioides,* both white- and pink-flowering forms, and the wiry *Hibbertia empetrifolia,* whose buttercup-yellow flowers light any shaded area.

Soon we crossed an old log bridge over a creek, which suddenly broadened out under a grove of *Leptospermum.* Leaving the track, we moved in under the tea-trees and within a few metres discovered our first patch of *Astelia,* growing in spongy soil. The strap leaves were silver and in older clumps were more than a metre long. I mentally compared this to the dwarf alpine species, *Astelia alpina,* relatively common on all mountains which hold winter snow. No flowers were evident on the flowering stalks which arose from the centre of the clustered leaves, but a number of fleshy orange seeds were. Not even the leeches which abounded in the moisture could deter us from admiring this striking plant which (except in a few similar, closely located habitats) is found nowhere else in Australia.

One has to cross the Tasman Sea to New Zealand to view this plant again. There it can be found on both the north and south islands, and Stewart Island. The plant was obviously a common component of the general landmass that connected New Zealand to Australia. It grows extensively in alpine and subalpine areas in New Zealand, where conditions are evidently very favourable. The drier, generally lower profile of Australia has forced it to retreat to a few suitable pockets, and even here it has suffered greatly from fire. Records indicate a great decline in the populations, which were small even then, after the disastrous 1939 fires.

Returning to the car, we drove down towards Powelltown, and quickly left the moist, tall forests behind us as we entered the more sclerophyll peppermint forests.

We realised how tenuous was the hold of many of the plants we had enjoyed that day in this changing environment. With constant pressure for land use, every effort must be made to ensure the survival of all elements that have limited habitat.

26 RIVERINA

NEW SOUTH WALES

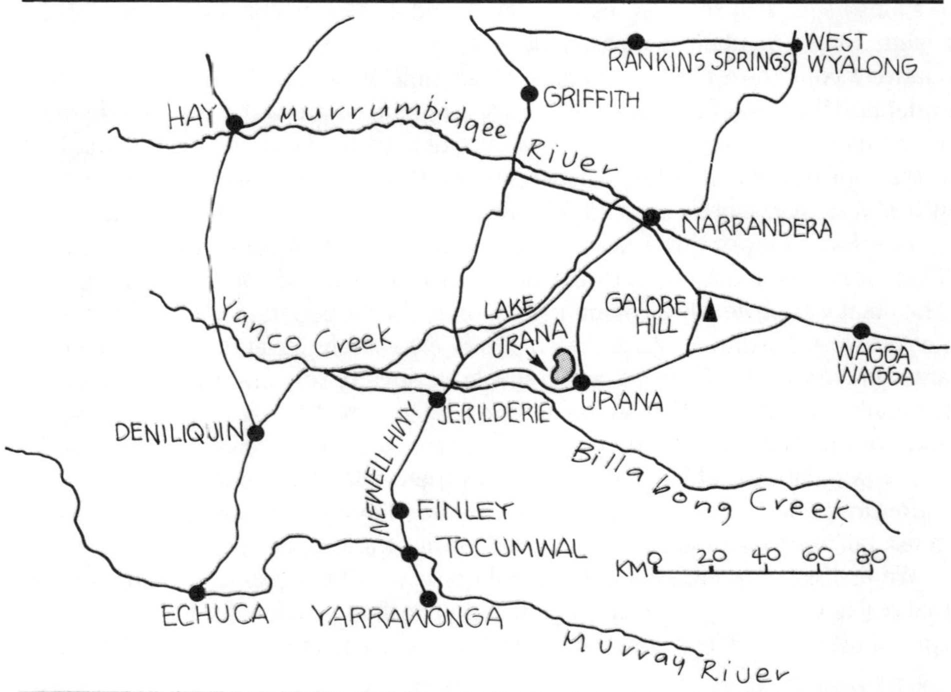

When driving along main arterial roads my attention is often arrested by a blaze of colour, or a dramatic change in the plant communities or the general topography. My instinct is always to stop and investigate. I am naturally curious about our environment, and more so when I am travelling through one that changes frequently or is new to me.

I have often found myself enthralled with a plant, not because it is new to me but because of the way it is growing. In one instance recently, while driving north of Dubbo, in NSW, it was *Pandorea pandorana*, the 'wonga vine'. It festooned every available tree and branch, climbing as high as 15 metres or more, draping all with its waxy pinnate foliage and profuse flowers, which are open-lipped trumpets, and in this case ranged from a pale to golden cream. As the flowers hung down, I could look up into their throats, which were either purple-streaked or had one or more lips coloured a bright orange. The individual flowers were no more than 2 centimetres across, but so effectively did they blanket the foliage that the amount of them could only be guessed at. Numerous white-eared honeyeaters were enjoying the free-flowing, sweetly perfumed nectar.

Having spent perhaps an hour exploring this area and the other plants it contained, we boiled our billy and sat within five or six metres of the road to enjoy our surroundings further. A large number of cars rushed by, many pulling caravans and obviously belonging to people on holidays. None stopped, and few appeared aware of the beauty around them. Yet if such a display had been in a garden or flower show the same people would have paid to see it.

We wondered what 'getting away' meant to these people who seemed in such a hurry. Was it simply a case of 'been there, done that' without any real interest in their surroundings? Do people drive from one town to the next, pausing perhaps to look at items prescribed by travel brochures, before parking in the local caravan park, their pre-planned destination for that night? This would seem to be so. Few people have any sense of adventure; they have allowed the unaffected curiosity of childhood to become lost in the busy practicality of their unimaginative lives. Would they care if natural forest or heathland no longer existed, if they drove only along highways flanked with open farmland and billboards announcing the attractions of the next town? It was a sobering thought.

The previous day we had spent driving through the Riverina. The topography of this vast riverine sandplain in southern New South Wales is altered only moderately in elevation by ancient mudstone and sandstone rises, and by the many rivers, streams and drainage lines which have etched their pathways deeply into the surface. Even so, there is great change in plant communities, with mallee, redgum flats, and *Callitris* pine communities being encountered over short distances.

Pine forests often stretch for many kilometres on either side of the road. This species, *Callitris columellaris*, is valued for its timber, which is used extensively for cabinet work as well as for buildings on rural properties. A perfume is given off by freshly cut wood, and when it is burnt the smoke has a distinctive sandalwood aroma. It is not a large tree, and it favours undulating or stony rise country. As we drove through forest after forest of the white cypress the temperature was sufficiently warm to induce the trees to transpire essential oils, and the perfume filled the car very pleasantly.

At the base of a number of these rocky hills, and in particular where deep sand and moisture collected, we found many hundreds of freshly germinating bulbs of *Calostemma purpurea*, the native daffodil, lying on top of the sand. These bulbs are the size of a large pea, and contain sufficient reserves of food to provide for the sprouting young plant. Moisture isn't of great consequence at this stage, and gradually the root penetrates deeply into the gritty red soil. In late spring the leaves ascend to about 30 centimetres and the flower stalks appear and rapidly grow from their base. The small yellow or deep pink-red flowers are held in loose clusters at the very top of this stem, and flower successively for some months. When all the buds have completed their cycle, the final bulbs drop to the ground and the leaves wither, leaving the parent bulb dormant in the ground.

The large-flowered, large-leaved *Crinum flaccidum*, which follows a similar perennial cycle, is most often found farther west. It is common above major waterways such as the Darling and Murray rivers.

Floristically, one of the most interesting areas in the Riverina is Galore Hill, situated almost midway between Narrandera and Wagga. It is like a sentinel in a flat plain, and its broad top and flanks are home to plants that occur also in Gippsland and northern NSW.

Galore Hill is the most southerly outpost for *Grevillea floribunda*, a shrub with soft grey foliage and bunches of yellow flowers covered in rusty hairs. It is commonly found on both granite and sandstone in areas around Coonabarabran, Mudgee and northwards into Queensland. It was earlier confused with the Victorian plant, *Grevillea chrysophaea*, of Gippsland and the Brisbane Ranges north of Geelong.

Three other plants, *Indigofera australis*, *Eriostemon myoporoides*, and *Hardenbergia violacea*, are found ranging over vast areas and in dramatically different habitats.

Indigofera is a light open shrub, with pinnate foliage and delicately perfumed sprays of pink or sometimes white pea flowers. It is transcontinental, and I have observed it growing in as widely disjunct areas as Carnarvon Gorge in Queensland, the Grampians in Victoria, and in southern Western Australia in a less than hospitable environment.

Hardenbergia violacea, another member of the pea family, is well known for its masses of purple or candy-pink flowers, its trailing or climbing habit, and its large leathery leaves, which people have sometimes confused with eucalyptus leaves. It is a plant commonly seen hanging down the face of road cuttings throughout south-eastern Australia where its massed flowering display, often combined with the gold or yellow of a wattle species, is one of the most striking bush combinations. It is a plant that favours drier rocky soils, and its habit of creeping about the floor of lightly shaded forests makes its appearance startlingly pleasurable.

Eriostemon myoporoides shows its versatility by being able to colonise, and adapt to habitats so diverse that you wonder if you are looking at the same plant. In Gippsland it occupies both dry rocky bluffs in low rainfall areas, where summer's sun scorches the rock, and cool forests in deep soils, which for part of the year are under snow. The most northerly area in which I have collected specimens is the sandy, often inundated Wallum scrub of near-coastal Queensland. Whereas the alpine forms from Falls Creek in Victoria may have leaves up to 10 centimetres long, those of the northern population are barely 1 centimetre, and the overall stature of the plant, which suckers freely, may be less than 30 centimetres.

Think of the forces and time and scale of evolution involved in these adaptations! I fear that some day we will bitterly regret the wholesale clearing of forests, plains, and heathlands. What a pity many of the sciences by which we are now starting to unlock the mysteries contained in our plants were not in existence at the time when these irreversible decisions were being made!

There is another aspect of the Riverina, different from the broad plains with their meandering creeks, or the low jump-ups on and around which the *Callitris* forests are often found: the mallee communities. These dominate large areas of undulating sand country in the southern part of the Riverina, or combine with other plant communities where soil types meet.

The main indicators of these interesting areas, which carry a diverse flora, are a dozen or more *Eucalyptus* species, some widespread, others more localised. *Eucalyptus dumosa*, with its interesting, ribbed buds and one of the largest individual flowers in this group, can be found over most of the sand plain country; and because of its compact, mostly multi-stemmed habit, and its adaptability, it has succeeded in gardens in a range of climates. The same is true of many mallees, and I have successfully grown most of these species from the drier, better drained areas in our heavier Melbourne soils.

Many of the eucalypts also occur in the mallee areas of western Victoria and in South Australia, and one, *Eucalyptus incrassata*, can be found in similar areas in Western Australia. All but one, *E. calycogona*, have white to cream flowers, none the less beautiful or appreciated by bees and birds because of their lack of colour. *E. calycogona* often has pink filaments, and even though the individual flowers are not large, they are numerous; a small tree of this fine-foliaged species is a soft haze of pink when in full flower.

I have always enjoyed investigating mallee heathland, as so much is happening either at eye level, or at your feet, the flowers and canopy of the mallee eucalypts and taller shrubs being only a scant metre or so above the smaller plants.

Small birds, insect or nectar feeding, can be seen moving from tree to tree or shrub at a level at which they are more readily seen and recognised. Binoculars are an essential accessory, as shyer birds may keep moving just out of a range where their markings can be seen.

A widespread bird commonly seen in south-eastern Australia, the white-eared honeyeater, inhabits heathlands and mallee as well as taller forests. It is an active bird of about 20 centimetres, with markings of yellow green above and a lighter toning of the same colours beneath. A bright yellow line runs below its eye, and the common name derives from a white patch behind its eye. The smaller, yellow-plumed honeyeater inhabits a mainly mallee habitat, and its other distinguishing marks are a streaked chest and belly, and a tuft of yellow feathers below the ear.

It is not only on the eucalypts that the small and not so small birds feed. There is an abundance of other nectar-bearing plants among which is a number of species of grevilleas, some wide spread, others localised. One of these is the needle-leaved *G. glabella*, a familiar and popular garden plant, found in the Riverina only around Rankin's Spring, but in similar habitats in Victoria and South Australia. Similarly, *G. ilicifolia*, while being found only about Nerican, is a major component of Victorian and South Australian mallee. Some forms have holly-like leaves, as the name suggests, and the bunches of pink or red flowers are popular sources of nectar.

The mid-level of these heathland communities is visually dominated by acacias when they are at the height of their flowering; and everywhere one gazes over a sea of lemon and yellow fluffy blossom. The one which always seems the brightest to me, though it is by no means confined to the mallee, is *Acacia decora*: a medium shrub with golden flowers set against glaucous, oblong foliage. Much taller, and with long, narrow, flexile leaves and bright yellow flowers is *Acacia rigens*, which, like all others, is such an important food source for a wide range of birds. One of the more unusual and seemingly imbalanced bird-plant relationships, is that between *Astroloma conostephioides* and the emus. This small member of the epacrid family has masses of red tubular flowers, rich in nectar. Emus seek out the combination of these and the plant's seeds; the sight of these large birds picking the flowers from numerous bushes with their large beaks is somewhat incongruous. These feeding patterns are readily detected by the droppings, which contain the discarded, now straw-coloured flowers.

You will often see a grass as the only plant growing under mallee eucalypts in the red soils; this is *Trioda irritans,* and it should be approached with caution, as its spine-like leaves are unyielding and very sharp. This plant, which can eventually cover many metres, has an unusual pattern of growth, dying out in the centre, but expanding outwards like a giant donut. The great area covered by some of these plants has often caused people flying over them to suggest that they were craters. I have often found kangaroos lying in the bare centres and having a dust bath. *Trioda irritans* is one of the many striking features of these complex plant communities, of which only a fraction now remains. It is great camping and walking country; and this is the only way really to learn to appreciate its intricacies.

27 KALBARRI

& MURCHISON RIVER WESTERN AUSTRALIA

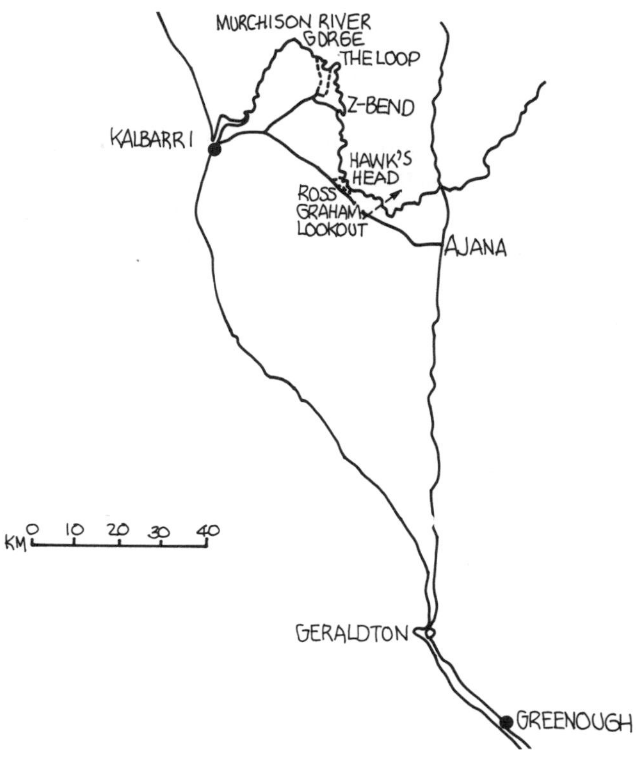

The Kalbarri sandplains through which the Murchison River runs – having etched its course deeply into ancient, uplifted sandstones – have a flora of great beauty and diversity. A number of species, one being *Melaleuca calothamnoides,* have southern counterparts; in this instance *Melaleuca lateritia,* which no doubt evolved from a common ancestor. Others, such as *Calothamnus quadrifidus,* can be found in both the southern and central coastal areas, as well as inland to the Stirling Range.

On our first spring trip to Kalbarri we found that the extensive sandplains of Ajana and Kalbarri, dry and hot even in mid-spring, carried many plants that have evolved and adapted to these harsh local conditions. An interesting aspect of these lateritic soils, which may not be fully recognised till much later, becomes apparent when you are perhaps looking at colour slides, or maybe when someone asks, 'What eucalypts grow there?' The answer is that eucalypts do not stand out here as they do on so many of the southern heathlands. It is other, smaller members of the Myrtaceae family, along with the Proteaceae, which are apparent: *Verticordia*, *Beaufortia*, *Baeckea*, *Thryptomene*, *Calothamnus*, *Calytrix*, and *Pileanthus* (the orange-flowering 'copper cups') seem to be everywhere. Pink, purple, yellow, tangerine, red, and white are the colours of the low fine structure which comprises the majority of this environment. Much of it does not reach above knee height, so that you are continually looking down at and across a sea of changing colour.

Interestingly, it was two white or creamy-white plants lining the road into Kalbarri National Park which caught our eye. One has the quaint, though understandable, local name of cauliflower bush, in this case northern cauliflower. The plant, which is a mounding shrub, and botanically known as *Verticordia polytricha*, certainly bears some similarity to the vegetable, but this is only an illusion. The effect is created by the mass of feathery cupped flowers which cover the foliage totally in their thousands. Their large white heads are scattered irregularly amongst the other species of these heathlands.

The second plant, *Grevillea leucopteris*, can only be described as grand. With a structural dominance that dwarfs all other plants around it, it is flamboyant and opportunistic, a large shrub with a number of branches radiating up from near the base. The leaves are large, soft, grey, and deeply lobed; so that even when not in flower it is handsome in appearance. From the midst of this foliage tall hairy branches rise into the air, and it is on these that the large cylindrical spikes of flowers eventually appear. When fully out, their weight causes the flowering branches to bend, waving gracefully in the slightest breeze.

Before flowering, the immature buds are surrounded by large woolly pink bracts which are themselves attractive and, after flowering, large sticky seed capsules complete the picture. Every aspect of this shrub is unusual, even the perfume of the flowers, which seems to be more attractive to flies than to traditional pollinating agents. Our most vivid memory of this plant was the sight, late one evening as we drove south-westward, of acre upon acre of them, their arching flower stems silhouetted blackly against the orange-tinged sunset sky.

Grevillea leucopteris is one of a group of grevilleas that exhibit this robustness and display their flowers on long, almost leafless branches. The better known two are *G. eriostachya* and *G. excelsior*, both with intense orange flower heads.

Only on these lower Murchison River sandheaths will you find *Grevillea annulifera*, a shrub with intricate rigid leaves and large heads of cream flowers. Some authors comment on the unpleasant smell, but I was so taken by the bright pink suffusing the cream of the flowers as they aged that I did not notice it.

Growing below this grevillea, *Beaufortia squarrosa* can often be found. It is a low spreading shrub with small bottlebrush flowers varying from honey-yellow to tangerine to red. These are rich in nectar, and a pressed specimen, which dropped out of a book I was looking through recently, still had traces of this sweet honey smell. As with many myrtles, the foliage is so fine or stem-clasping that it is fairly inconspicuous, particularly when the flowers are so prolific that they completely cover the plant.

Pileanthus peduncularis, and some possibly closely related new species, have bright orange tea-tree flowers with dark purple centres. They are mostly small undershrubs, which poke through the stems of more vigorous plants, confusing the beholder by presenting their bright buttons amongst other flowers.

Verticordias in most cases have flowers that dominate and frequently cover their fine aromatic foliage. They have earned their common name of feather flowers both from the way in which the calyx lobes are finely divided, and from the feathery appendages that are prominent on many species and are situated at the base of the calyx. These are often the same colour as the primary lobes, but sometimes they provide an interesting contrast to the main colour. It is a gay and generally colourful genus ranging through a full spectrum from white to purple.

Verticordia chrysostachys, a brilliant yellow-flowering species, was only halfway into full flower, but the potential beauty of this small shrub was even then very obvious. Unlike *V. polytricha*, this species does not have a cauliflower appearance, but carries its flowers along upright twiggy stems, with flowers opening from the base toward the apex, some being fully out before maximum bud development at the tip has taken place.

Verticordias, with few exceptions, have proved difficult in cultivation, being intolerant of dense soils that hold water. Some success has been had by growing them in containers in very open soil mediums, and with little in the way of fertilisers. Because of their beauty, this inability to tame them has caused much frustration; but no doubt, with grafting techniques now being employed more, many of them will find their way onto hardier stocks.

Every new ridge or depression brings the joy of new discovery, and Kalbarri really is a wonderland of wildflowers. It is in sharp contrast to the bed of the Murchison River itself, which we dropped down into from a tongue of land formed by a broad loop in the river, spending a whole day wandering along the sandy edge.

The cliff faces in many parts are roughly like steep, narrow-treaded staircases, and perched on these, nibbling at whatever herbage is available, are small herds of feral goats. They eat just about everything they find, and their ability to negotiate these narrow tracts on steep faces produces a constant rattle as stones are dislodged and roll into the river far below. In such an environment – which is dry, with little in the way of soil-binding vegetation – these introduced animals are destroying the plants and creating severe problems of soil erosion.

At various points along the river we were greeted by a sight familiar to us in the east but encountered for the first time in the west: a callistemon growing along the edge of a broad waterway. There are only two species of bottlebrush in Western Australia: this one, *Callistemon phoenicius*, which we knew well from moist flats and annual drainage channels farther south; and the beautiful *C. speciosus*, so prolific around Albany, again on swampy ground, or, like the eastern *C. pallidus*, often occupying granite hills. *C. phoenicius* has grey leaves rather sparsely set on angular branches, and brilliant scarlet brushes, the first of which were just opening on some of these plants.

The other plant that made us feel at home was *Eucalyptus camaldulensis*, the river red gum found on rivers throughout Australia, and occasionally, paradoxically, on rocky hilltops. The trees grew right to the water's edge and, as we could see by the blackened marks up their grey trunks and the debris caught in lower branches, were seasonally inundated, as they are throughout most of their range. As they age and lose branches, hollows develop by weathering in the stump of the branch, creating perfect nesting sites for many species of parrots. The name 'parrot' is a loose terminology, covering as well as parrots, rosellas, budgerigars, corellas, cockatoos, lorikeets, the galah and the cockatiel. Often their nests are so precarious, or the young so active, that they tumble into the water. In eastern states this is the reason why Murray Cod cruise a beat below a stretch of red gums and spend much time tucked into submerged roots. There is probably a counterpart in these western rivers that takes advantage of the misadventures of nestlings.

We had noticed numerous patches of salt on rocks above the normal water level, and realised that we were wise to have brought fresh water with us. It was well over 40°C. down in the valley, with a blinding glare reflecting off the water, sand and cliff walls. We nevertheless tasted the Murchison water and were not surprised to find that, like most south-western rivers, it had an appreciably high salt level. We surmised that either the vegetation had adapted to this level or the salt level was still within its range of tolerance.

That evening, having bathed in the salty river, we made our way back downstream and climbed the still-hot cliffs to our vehicle. It was just on dark, and ours was the only vehicle left. We were just about to leave when a distressed hiker appeared. She was one of a group of relatively inexperienced walkers who had left their car much farther upstream, and had taken two days to walk a distance they had been told would take them slightly more than a day. Not knowing the river was not suitable for drinking water, they had only taken sufficient water for the shorter trip. Our presence saved them some distress and inconvenience, since their vehicles were 25 kilometres away.

This country can never be taken lightly, for it will inevitably catch you out. If these people had been in an even more remote area the consequences of their bad preparation could have been disastrous.

The last day of our stay at Kalbarri was spent on the sea cliffs at the mouth of the Murchison River. The cliffs not only contained a marvellous collection of plants, but revealed ancient records, held locked in their cemented sands, of past marine activity. High up on cliff faces some 20 metres above water level, like pipes of an organ, the casts of a now extinct giant marine worm sit vertically on the exposed rock. They are only one indicator of a once much higher sea-level, for the platform on which we were standing was one of a series running back down to the water like giant steps.

In their shape you could read the story of a receding sea cutting fresh platforms as its level dropped. It was probably during the same, or a similar period that the gradually uplifting Murchison sandstones were being deeply cut by the river – a period covering several million years.

For all its vastness and plant diversity, Kalbarri exhibits a fragile quality, as dry sand plains so often do. As with much of Australia, you become lulled into a false sense of there being such vast areas of land that the alienation of a little more won't matter. 'She's a big country mate!'

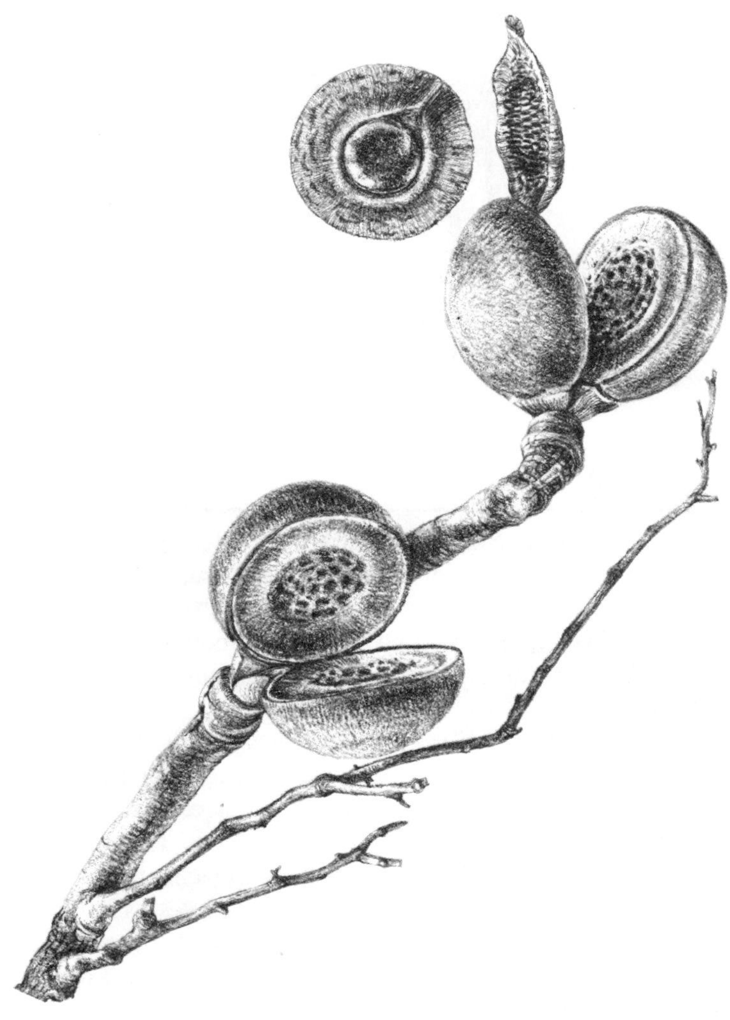

Hakea platysperma

28 DONGARA TO JURIEN BAY

WESTERN AUSTRALIA

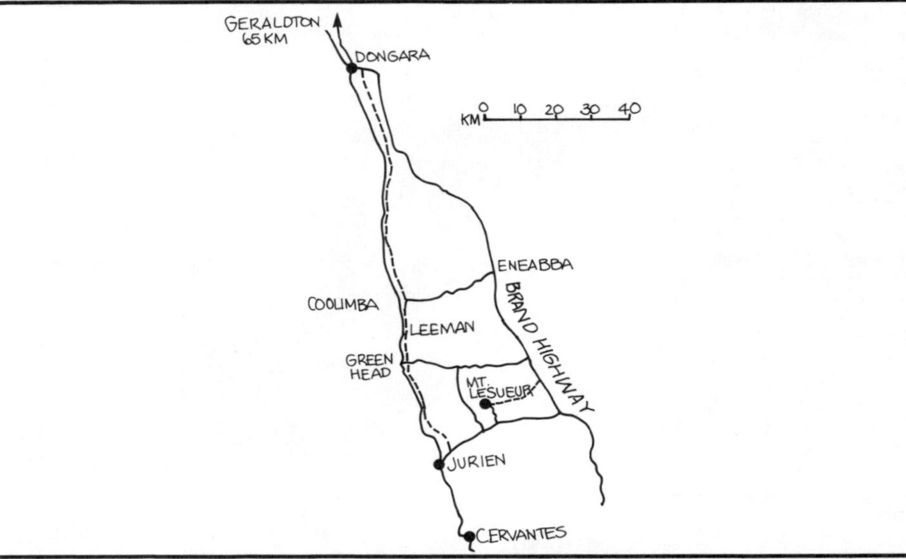

In a genus in which many species exhibit large or odd-shaped buds and seed capsules, *Eucalyptus erythrocorys* is one of the most unusual. The specific name appropriately translates to 'red helmet', an allusion to the bright red bud cap and its shape. When this cap is forced off by the expanding stamens, and they open out, they display fully the brilliant golden yellow colouring for which the flowers are renowned.

Strangely, in all my trips to the West I had not ever seen it in its natural habitat, nor had I spoken to anyone who knew it. We knew that it occurred on limestone south of Dongara about 65 kilometres south of Geraldton, and below Greenough, a historic settlement where another unusual eucalypt grows. That one is actually a form of *E. rudis,* which grows in almost horizontal east-facing poses in response to constant westerly winds. Saplings and large ancient trees with thick trunks all exhibit this tendency – which on a still, calm day looks paradoxical.

I have asked many people about the forces that could create this unique situation, but none has been able to give a definite answer. One suggestion was that the wind was so strong that a wind-sheer effect knocked off the buds on the windward side, so that only branches on the lee side could grow. But if this were so, how, I wondered, could anyone live in and farm this area?

There is a second interesting phenomenon: at the mouth of the Greenough River there is a lake suspended in sand-dunes, a geomorphological feature that is very strange. I wondered whether perhaps the same force had played a part in shaping both the dunes and the growth habit of *E. rudis*. I am trying to obtain seed from this leaning eucalypt to see how offspring behave in a normal environment.

Leaving Dongara, we turned onto the coast road instead of continuing on the more inland road, and within 5 kilometres, on a limestone ridge to our right, we spotted a group of the tell-tale smooth white trunks of *Eucalyptus erythrocorys*.

As we climbed towards the crown of the ridge, we passed through groves of one of the shapeliest grevilleas we have encountered. It was *G. argyrophylla*, which was dark-trunked and had a uniform rounded canopy of 5-6 metres in height. In appearance it reminded us of an olive tree, so dark green was the foliage, but on most shrubs this was smothered by heads of white flowers. There are not many grevilleas that grow on limestone or calcareous soils, most favouring acid to neutral conditions.

As we passed through these dark grevillea groves, the eucalypts came into full view and we both expressed surprise at their generally small stature. Many had multi-trunks, almost mallee-like, except that there was no ligno-tuber present, and the tallest tree was about 6 metres. Although none was in flower, flowering being in Autumn, the large angular seed capsules, both old and fresh green, indicated how profuse this can be.

We have had difficulty in establishing this attractive tree in Melbourne's dense clay, and I realised, looking at its natural habitat, why it looked so much at home and so vigorous on the limestone-derived sands of Perth and Adelaide.

Shortly after leaving this rewarding find, we chanced upon a second, smaller track that evidently followed the coast even more closely than the road we were on. This would take us above Cockleshell Gully into the bottom end of Mt Lesueur, our next major destination. Like so many interesting tracks, this one was used mainly by local farming folk and fishermen; being on the rough side, such roads tend to discourage general traffic. While there was some open farmland, there were still extensive reserves of natural bushland.

Most of the area was comprised of calcareous dunes, with the dense low vegetation successfully binding this light sand against wind erosion. We saw many plants, including the rare *Grevillea olivacea*, a second plant that has the leaf form of the European olive (this time with red flowers); but three plants in particular made this diversion worthwhile.

Two were growing together on a regenerated rise on farmland. The first of these, *Billardiera ringens*, I have grown for many years as a light to medium climber. It has glossy mid-green ovate leaves and orange-red bell flowers in bunches. In this particular spot, we found it growing as a dense mounding shrub, about 60 centimetres high and nearly 2 metres across, with the bunches of lustrous flowers sitting all over the green hummock like so many orange posies. While we were enjoying and photographing this find, we spied compact, small bushes farther up the slope, with pink and white flowers dotted over them. We recognised the plant as *Pimelea ferruginea*, a common component of granite coastal heathlands of the south-west corner, just below Busselton. My older books did not list it growing so far north, but it is the same plant, though a paler-flowered form, that has for so long been a horticultural favourite.

We had spent so much time enjoying our slow drive on this old track that, as often happens, we had to scramble to find a camp site before darkness set in. Fortunately, numerous tracks led through the dunes to the ocean beach and, taking a likely one, we wound around and over the dunes until we found a level tucked-away spot, sheltered from the cool evening wind.

As soon as we alighted we were greeted by a familiar plant, *Calothamnus quadrifidus*, the widest spread of the net bush family. Instead of the usual large shrub, this population was totally prostrate, in full flower, and hanging over and down the steep cutting formed by the track. We didn't immediately recognise it for two reasons: firstly, its prostrate habit; secondly, it was liberally covered with the fine limestone dust that cast a light mantle over any plants within its drift pattern. As I found from my first trip across the old Nullarbor road, there is no dust so invasive as bull-dust, as it is locally known. The large, lustrous, red claw-tipped brushes were almost light grey, so thickly were they covered, as was the soft needle foliage. As with old treasures in an attic, a good dusting revealed the hidden beauty beneath.

As we were dusting, and then photographing, a small bird darted out from beneath the canopy of foliage. We thought we recognised it as a red-browed pardalote, and looked for and found the tunnel hole in the bank that led to its nest. It is a dainty bird with distinct white spotting, and brown and black markings. In the eastern states I have seen pardalotes building nesting tunnels in soil which may have been deposited only a few days. While we were not certain of the identity of this particular pardalote, as again from our books it appeared to be out of its range, the other species common in the area, the 'striated pardalote', frequents trees and their hollows.

Next morning we moved gradually back inland and, leaving the limestone country behind, came again into sandplain and laterite and to a profusion of flowers, which is so often the case with this habitat. There seemed to be so much of everything in this complex heathland, that it was almost pointless attempting to pick out too many individual species. With certainty, though, one could say that two families, Proteaceae and Myrtaceae, were the strongest components. *Grevillea, Dryandra, Hakea, Conospermum, Banksia, Isopogon, Petrophile*, and *Lambertia*, the major protead members, were all present; while *Baeckea, Thryptomene, Melaleuca, Darwinia, Calothamnus* and *Calytrix* ensured that the myrtles were well represented.

It is a revealing and awe-inspiring living classroom where, within a few square metres, you can study millions of years of evolution. The differences between, say, *Grevillea* and *Hakea*, or *Isopogon* and *Petrophile*, are not great; but when you compare each to, say, *Conospermum*, the extreme evolutionary paths can be appreciated.

In our preoccupation, Sue and I had wandered in different directions, she having made her way to a higher plain 100 metres or so away. As I came near she was simply standing in what appeared to be, from my position, a hillside of *Anigozanthos humilis*, and *A. pulcherrimus*, as well as many of the plants we had seen just a few minutes earlier. Within a few more yards I realised, as she had at that point, that the whole area had been ripped, probably late on the previous day. Already many plants with their roots fully exposed were wilting, and as the sun, still low in the early morning sky, increased its intensity, so did more plants wilt under stress.

Sue was shedding a silent tear for this – and no doubt all previously totally destroyed areas of beauty. And as we drove away in our own silence I wondered just how little would be left in ten years.

Over the time I have been journeying to the West, I have seen a dramatic reduction in the areas of sandplain flora. It is unfortunate that this country is favoured for cropping or grazing. Many of the once extensive floral areas are now confined only to weed-infested road verges or gravel scrapes, places where viability, both physically and genetically, is constantly threatened. It was only a few kilometres on that we found such a situation, and those few patches of plants that did still exist showed what beauty this area must previously have offered.

In this instance one plant was the major component, this being *Xanthosia tomentosa*, the northern Southern Cross. This is a trailing, matting, softly foliaged shrub, whose 'flowers' are made up mainly of large soft pink or yellow bracts. It is such an attractive plant that, even where it grew in association with the red or orange of *Lechenaultia* or the vivid blue of *Dampiera*, it conceded nothing to them.

From here we could make out the low laterite ranges, a part of which was Mt Lesueur, north-west of Jurien Bay. This was to be our destination for camp that evening, an area I had visited frequently, though not for ten years. I have some extremely fond memories of Mt Lesueur, in the discovering of plants confined to this floristically rich area. We picked up familiar landmarks and dropped into the head of a gully to set up camp under the first tall eucalypts that we had seen for some days.

These were *Eucalyptus accedens*, the northern wandoo or Powderbark, a tall tree of 20 or more metres, with clean white trunks covered in a waxy powder or bloom. Little grew beneath them, and an open parkland appearance was the result. Nearer the dry creek edge, or where the ground was more open, *Grevillea biternata*, an arching shrub with fine lacy foliage, often purple tipped, and with delicate white flowers to match, grew in low colonies. With them grew an occasional *Chorizema cordatum*, a small shrub with toothed leaves and masses of orange-yellow pea flowers; and *Diplolaena microcephala*, the smallest flowering member of a small genus with unusual pendant flowers.

Just to get a feel again of the landscape before night set in, we walked back up onto the heathland, where the structure of the plant communities changed dramatically to dwarf proportions.

With first light we arose and left camp with a day pack, for the only way to enjoy this country is on foot.

Soon we were recalling previous finds and, since this was our first spring trip, we saw much in flower that had previously been difficult to identify. *Conospermum* or smoke bushes often hold their small grey or white flowers above the fine foliage en masse: from a distance, a large group in flower certainly does give the appearance of smoke. Here, however, we found a species with blue flowers, a colour not often seen in the Proteaceae family to which they belong. This was *C. nervosum,* a shrub of a metre with grey-green leaves and umbels of blue flowers at the ends of the stems.

Growing near by was the widespread *Isopogon divergens,* with loose pink 'mophead' flowers and narrowly divided lobed foliage. The uninitiated would certainly find it difficult to place this plant in the same family as 'smoke bush'.

On the edge of the track, in white sand, grey trailing stems with little foliage bore the large bright red flowers of *Lechenaultia hirsuta*, tangling with the equally grey-foliaged and related *Scaevola phlebopetala*. The difference in colour between these two is startling: while the colour of the *Lechenaultia* could only be said to be blood red, that of the *Scaevola* was royal purple. Against the pure white sand or overlying the orange laterite, such combinations are remarkable, and put a lie to the often made statements regarding the lack of colour in our flora.

One of the plants endemic to this region is *Hakea megalosperma,* which has one of the smallest flowers in the genus and, paradoxically, one of the largest seed pods. These are often 7 centimetres long and, like many hakeas, have hornlike appendages at one end. When picked, or after fire, these pods separate into two woody halves, dispelling the black winged seed.

We spent the whole day just wandering in this manner, finding new plants wherever a different aspect or slope presented itself. The rare *Banksia tricuspis,* a large shrub with fine soft leaves, was not in flower, but was covered in new shiny green seed pods. Having previously seen this plant in flower, we well remembered the brilliance of its lemon brushes.

Two melaleucas, one large and one very small, grew together and presented an interesting contrast. The larger, *Melaleuca tricophylla,* grows to 2 metres and has soft hairy foliage. The flowers are in one-sided brushes rather than balls or spikes, and firstly open cream in colour. As they begin to age the older parts become suffused in pink, presenting an attractive two-coloured effect. I am still trying to acclimatise it to Melbourne's wet, cold winters. *Melaleuca scabra,* the second plant, was only centimetres high and less than 30 centimetres across. This plant also has fine hairy leaves, but these were all but covered by the deep pink rounded flower heads. It is a spectacular small display and, paradoxically, it grows much better in colder climates than *M. tricophylla*.

As we made our way to camp, using an old track which was intersected by secondary tracks, we were approached by a vehicle. This was our first and only contact with people for the day, and they stopped for a chat. It transpired that the occupants, two men, worked for the State Government as vermin controllers

– in this instance, dingoes. We were casually asked where we had walked, and our reply brought the comment that we should keep away from the track intersection corners, since traps were buried on most of these. Almost as casually, we were informed that the teeth of the traps were smeared with strychnine.

On the eastern margin of this pristine area, we now found that several grazing properties had replaced the bushland in the decade since my last visit. The dingoes were naturally attracted to the lambs, and pressure to control them was now being exerted. We watched where we put our feet from then on, and left the area early next morning, happy at having revisited this beautiful place, but saddened at the thought of its possible further alienation.

As we drove eastward to the main highway we passed through a patch of *Sphaerolobium vimineum*, a small, often single-stemmed shrub with bright red and yellow pea flowers from top to bottom. It is one of the ancient heathland components, occurring across the continent into the mallee of Victoria. To us it was a further illustration of the time scale involved in evolutionary processes. An hour on a bulldozer could obliterate these millions of years of evolution.

Banksia laracina

29 QUOIN HEAD

WESTERN AUSTRALIA

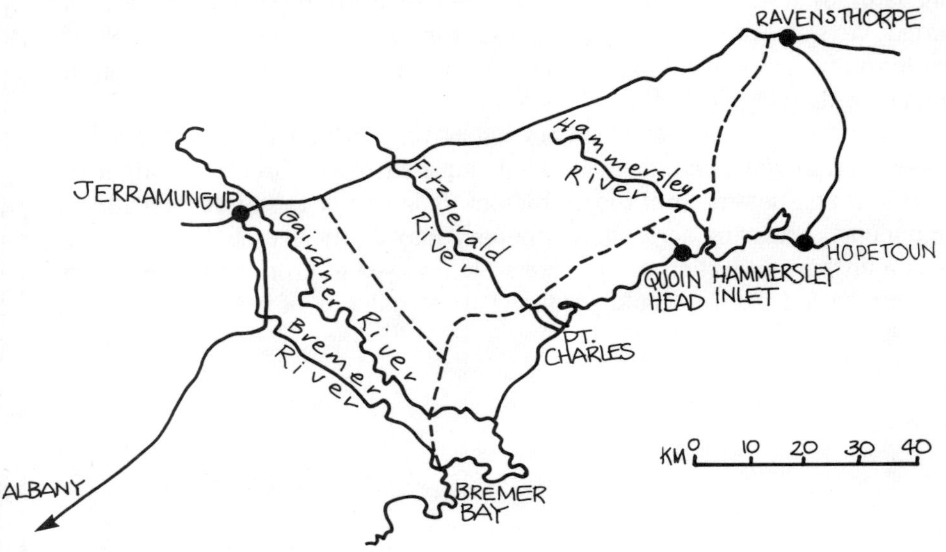

The central coastal parts of the Fitzgerald River National Park in southern Western Australia are areas of great contrast where changes of geology, aspect, and altitude have produced a wide diversity in the vegetation. Here, where many ancient islands of a previously higher sea-level are visible now as mountain ranges, numbers of individual species evolved in isolation.

On an earlier visit to the Barren Ranges (as this area is known) I had reached towards the centre ranges only from the eastern end. It was here that I had first seen the rare and beautiful *Eucalyptus sepulcralis*. A rugged range in the far distance had beckoned me farther until a very deep river crossing halted the progress of our vehicle. I left the area, with the distant majesty of these ranges, known as the Whoogerups, disappearing with a setting sun. I promised I would return to explore the country around and beyond this range.

Two and a half years elapsed, with the outline of the Whoogerups as clear as ever in my mind. A snap decision in November meant an opportunity to spend a week before Christmas with friends at remote Quoin Head on the coastal side of these ranges of distant mystery. Here, our camp site on a high headland was set in a protective copse of *Melaleuca acerosa*. It was the only plant of any height on this wind-shorn cliff head, and proved to be a splendid wind-break, as it is in many such areas far from its natural habitat.

Dwarf mallee heath community on Mt Lesueur, inland from Jurien Bay, WA. *Eucalyptus drummondii* is the only plant of any size and is only two metres high

Four compact plants that thrive in Mt Lesueur's lateritic sands. Top left, *Tetratheca sp.,* a small cascading plant more flower than foliage. Deep pink pom-pom flowers hide the fine hairy foliage of the dwarf sand-dweller below it, *Melaleuca scabra.* Top right: *Sphaerolobium vimineum.* This leafless sub-shrub stands out like a beacon in knee-high heathland. Transcontinental, it grows in mallee heathland in Victoria, as well as Western Australia. Below right, the compact large shrub *Melaleuca tricophylla,* with soft hairy foliage over which the bicolourous flowers bunch. The yellow are fresh, the pink the ageing flowers

The Whoogerup Range rises behind Quoin Head. On and around this range and the Hammersley Inlet in the foreground, isolated pockets of rare plants occur

The beach below was crescent-shaped, a broad white stretch of sand derived from the white, shining quartzite rock of which much of the area is comprised. This material, waxy-white in appearance, was formed when sandstones were subjected to tremendous pressures and heat in some ancient time, fusing them into a hard mass. Tilting, folding, and weathering have now transformed them into ranges, ridges, gullies, and shelves. It is on the sides of the gullies, where rain, wind, and heat have weathered out the less resistant rock, that many of the interesting plants occur. More moisture, lower temperatures, and protection from fierce salt-heavy winds have meant the creation of substantial, tall shrub communities, lusher than the hardened plants above on the exposed headlands.

So often in these situations one plant stands apart because of a specific difference in structure or colour. Such a one is *Regelia velutina*. This genus, a part of the 'bottlebrush' or Myrtaceae complex, grows only among the rocks of the Barrens. Its rich crimson flowers, though not overly large, could be seen from a great distance because of their intensity of colour. The growth habit of this shrub, which grows to 3 metres, is open and erect; and though it may appear rigid the silver foliage, so individual in this environment, imparts an immediate softness. The overall appearance is a velvety pewter grey or argentine, and this brightens and attracts from a distance as it catches the light reflected from the white rock around. It may be thought that such a plant could be difficult to grow on our eastern freeboard. In well drained soils it is not; but many have been disappointed waiting for it to flower.

Growing beneath the *Regelia*, as well as on cliffs exposed to the flattening force of the wind, is a plant more familiar as a rounded, 5-metre-high shrub. This is *Melaleuca nesophila*, a popular white-trunked paperbark with pink-purple pom-pom flowers in summer. In contrast to the *Regelia*, its leaves are round and a shiny dark green. It has adapted to this area by developing an almost prostrate, very spreading habit up to 3 metres across and barely 30 centimetres high. A third member of the Myrtaceae, *Beaufortia schaueri*, a small heath-like shrub with pink-mauve flowers, was in bloom on the heathlands. It retains its compact habit in cultivation and is a plant useful for both small gardens and containers.

In this area so rich in eucalypts of rare and unusual form one of the more widespread is *Eucalyptus preissiana*, aptly called the 'bell-fruited mallee'. It has sufficient differences to make it an oddity in a group which consists mostly of tall trunking trees or large shrubs. Even when grown away from here, the habit attained is still that of a low, scrambling shrub. On the specimens we encountered the large bright yellow flowers were very evident against the thick blue-grey leaves. Its habit suggests that it could be used not only as a garden specimen but for hedgerows and small stock shelter in lower rainfall areas.

One item you should not forget, when going to many southern Western Australian coastal areas, is fresh water – as much as you require for the duration of your stay, or until you visit a replenishing point. Water in streams is mostly too salty to drink, even a kilometre back from the coast and 40 metres above sea level. It is salt deposited by seas that covered these areas many times, salt now leaching out of the soil and being carried back to the sea via the many perennial and annual waterways that etch winding pathways to the coast. These large quantities of salt are held at a reasonable depth in the gravelly soils by the mallee or transitional woodlands that cover them. When these are removed (an occurrence on the increase) the salt rises to the surface with ground moisture, and there it stays after the moisture evaporates. It is unusual to find an occasional fresh water spring, such as the one we discovered on high ground behind our camp. It must have had its source deep below the rock; for it welled up without a trace of salt, yet within 50 metres it joined a second stream whose water was distinctly saline.

On one occasion, while we were enjoying a refreshing drink from a small pool formed by the spring, we witnessed a small fine-legged spider perform an interesting feat. It was poised on a sedge with a few of its long legs resting on the surface of the water. As we came closer, it slipped beneath the surface of the water running down the submerged part of the sedge. None of the party had witnessed this method of hiding before, and we all lay on our stomachs peering into the clear, still water, to see what the now submarine spider would do. What we saw was a fascinating adaptation we would never have imagined. The little fugitive was perhaps 10 centimetres under the water, clinging to the sedge; but what really caught our attention was that it had taken its own air supply down with it. This was in the form of quite large bubbles, which were clinging to a number of its legs; and by this means it was able to stay under water for at least the 15 minutes while we watched. The bubbles were also in contact with its body, but we were unsure by which avenue the oxygen found its way into the spider's body.

Our main concern was with botanising, so we continued our walk and did not return to the pool again for some hours. The spider was back on the sedge above the water, but dived beneath the surface as soon as we came too close.

Again we peered into the pool, and again it had bubbles attached to its legs. The light was less direct now and we were able to determine that the bubbles seemed to be caught on hairs on the spider's legs.

For Sue and me this was a discovery and a new experience. We did not have the means to collect and preserve a specimen, but no doubt some of these small arachnids, with their unusual evasive technique, will still be there on our next trip.

On the way out to Jerramungup we passed stands of both forms of what was originally known as *Eucalyptus lehmanni* or bushy yate. One has been referred to as the 'dwarf form' since it was smaller in all aspects than the traditional large shrub or tree form. The two have now been reclassified and, to add further confusion, the dwarf form, which grows only a few metres in height, has taken the specific name *lehmanni*. The original bushy yate – which, because of its habit, will no doubt retain this popular name – will from now on be known as *Eucalyptus conferruminata*.

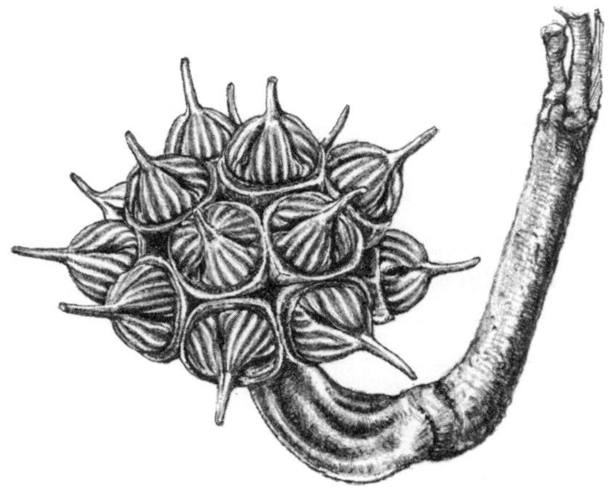

This lengthy but appropriate name has an interesting translation and history. As a point of explanation, these eucalypts are the only two to have fused aggregated seed capsules. When the mass of bright yellow-green flowers have withered, they leave behind a collection of capsules with long narrow protruding segments. As the seeds ripen, large pores open to shed them from the pendant fruits, and one's imagination can conjure up a whole lot of strange Bosch-like faces peering out from the drying capsule. They must have seemed like faces in torment to the modern botanists who bestowed the name, because the specific name *conferruminata* translates roughly to 'crowded together'. Botanical history now reveals that this quaint name was suggested for the plant by an author some time in the last century.

Whatever their status, both of these attractive eucalypts have been grown successfully on many windswept coastlines across southern Australia. I find great satisfaction in thinking about remote areas such as Quoin Head. Inevitably, it is the plants I use in my everyday work that take my mind back to these areas of such great peace.

30 SNOWY RIVER

VICTORIA

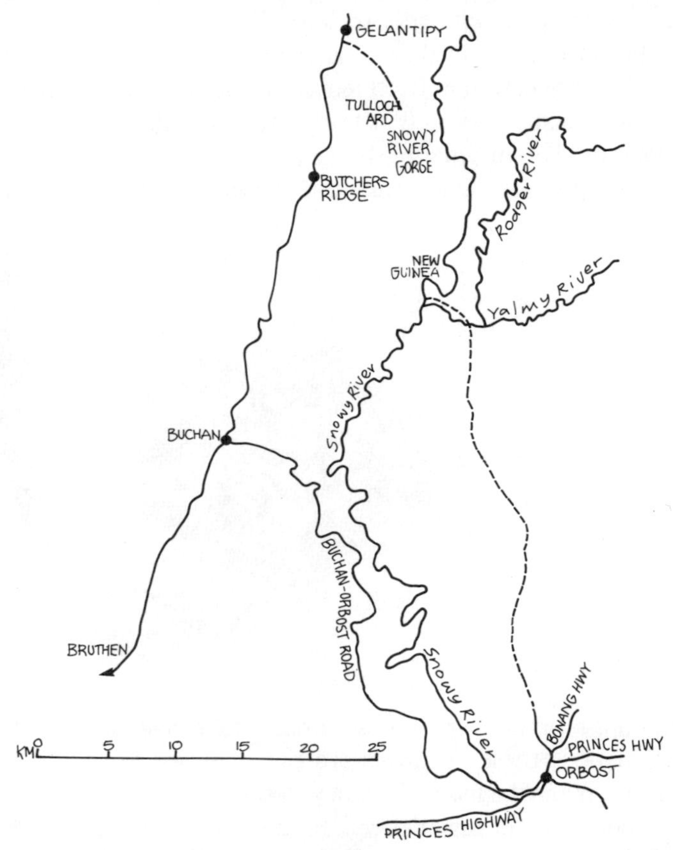

I used to wonder why so many Western Australians seemed to have so little appreciation for the floral beauty at their back doors, and why so few Sydneysiders seemed to know and appreciate the Hawkesbury sandstone areas. I used to pride myself on knowing the countryside of Victoria intimately, from the broad plains of the high country to the old dunes on which the western desert flora grows. But perhaps through tight schedules or a sense of adventure blunted by a troublesome lower back I tended to stick to familiar roads and tracks rather than to try new ones.

After re-reading that great naturalist, the late Norman Wakefield, I realised just how little I knew of the middle reaches of the Snowy River. I had spent time at the source of this beautiful river, below Kosciusko's summit, and on its upper and lower reaches, but had not seen any of its most spectacular stretch – the Snowy River Gorge, in particular the Tullach Ard section. So I decided to investigate these areas of the river, starting on the western bank at the southern end of the recently proclaimed Snowy River National Park. We intended to set up camp 50 kilometres north of Orbost by mid-afternoon; but, inevitably, patches of interesting bushland caught our eye and made us linger.

I have often found myself all but apologising to people for the lack of perfume in Australian plants. But there is no need to do this. At one stop the scent of *Acacia terminalis* in full flower was, we decided, a blending of lemon and spices. This early flowering small wattle always evokes memories of past autumns, and so, too, did the *Epacris impressa*, a tangle of pink, red, and white growing beneath them.

We eventually set up camp 30 metres above the Snowy River where, some kilometres below the gorge, it is a mostly broad, shallow river gliding over a fine sandy bottom. Footprints along the river told of wallabies, emus, dingoes, and goannas.

Directly opposite where we dropped down from our camp to the river was a weathered and very distorted limestone cliff, perhaps 60 metres high. This in itself was a beautiful spectacle, and crowning it, on slopes of 45 degrees, were hundreds of the most ancient *Xanthorrhoea* or grass trees. Everything – aspect, slope, drainage, and habitat – was just right for them, and we imagined the riot of noise from the hundreds of honeyeaters that would descend on them during their spring flowering. The isolation of this population of grass trees illustrates the need to investigate all remote and sometimes unlikely areas in order to discover and enjoy our marvellous plant heritage.

The following day we walked down and across the Snowy and up one of its tributaries, the Rodger River. We boiled the billy along the Rodger and, after lunch, headed upstream to its gorge, a narrow defile cut deep into ancient rock. Our path was barred by a long deep pool and we climbed the steep right bank to look down into the gorge. In this harsh rocky environment we found a dense though limited population of *Crowea exalata*, popular in its many forms in horticulture.

After pausing to admire this small fine-leaved, pink-flowering shrub, we continued to a position from which we could look down into the gorge. On returning, we kept to a contour perhaps 10–15 metres above the one on which we climbed, but saw no further sign of the *Crowea*. Nor did we see it again for the rest of our trip. This hardy plant is widespread but seldom plentiful, and I have seen it growing in such widely separated localities as the Whipstick near Bendigo, the Bluff in the Alps, and on coastal headlands.

As with many of our pristine waterways, much of the banks are choked by blackberries. This indomitable weed with delicious fruits, commonly referred to, perhaps unfairly, as von Mueller's curse, has crept like a cancer into many of the less accessible corners of Victoria.

Ferdinand von Mueller, Australia's most famous early botanist, supposedly scattered plant seeds on one of his many solo trips. He is said to have done this to provide some food in an environment that offered little in the way of food plants – at least to white man. When one reads authoritative works on *Rubus* (blackberry) and sees the variation in species and populations it seems difficult to lay the full responsibility at the feet of this brilliant, lonely man. None of this is of any help, though, when your pathway to a desirable section of a river is blocked by a wall of tangled prickles 3 metres tall and 8 metres wide.

If there are long, sturdy logs lying by, and sufficient strong people to manoeuvre them, these can be thrown on top of the blackberries. Their weight and yours, as you tread a precarious path along the logs, batters the weed down enough to allow you to cross over. We were continually frustrated in our attempts to approach the waters of the Snowy and its tributaries, being unable to find suitable logs and baffled by blackberry blockades.

As we sat enjoying a rest and observed the tracks and droppings of wombats, we noticed a well-worn pad disappearing into the base of a tangle of berries. On looking closer, we found this helpful wombat had pushed a pathway right through the tangle to gain access to the river. And so, with a minimal amount of prickling, we were able to wriggle along his pathway down to the water's edge. We found these pads were to provide access to the rivers more than once.

Since we wanted to see the section above the gorge, we left the lower Snowy and returned to Orbost, where we crossed the river and headed up the western side via Buchan, W Tree and Butchers Ridge. Here we branched off to the east to gain access to the steep slopes above the Snowy Gorge via the old Tullach Ard homestead.

We displaced a family group of emus to make camp, but they soon lost their shyness and stayed more or less in the vicinity. Early next morning we were able to drop down from here into the head of the Tullach Ard section of the gorge. Here, in contrast to our previous camp, the river was narrow, deep and fast, cutting deeply into the old volcanic rock – believed in some parts to be nearly 3 kilometres thick. Debris caught on rocks, sometimes 25 metres above the present waterline, indicated what a torrent this now serene river could be in full flood.

It was the rock structures, sculptured and polished into glassy smoothness by millions of years of water flow, that dominated this landscape. One area of gleaming black ancient slate was like ebony to the touch. Dwarf forms of *Acacia boormanii*, only a metre high and in bud, were growing in rock crevices. Its common name of Snowy River wattle indicates that this lovely shrub, well known in horticulture, is almost limited in its natural occurrence to the river tracts. Unfortunately, the length of time it takes to climb into and out of the gorge (around five hours) leaves little time for full investigation of the whole gorge and its sheer cliffs in just one day.

The country above the river contains many interesting and often locally limited plants. One of these, *Boronia ledifolia*, is limited to two small Victorian areas, although common in New South Wales. We saw it the next day, growing at the

top of a cliff face and, like many plants here, it seemed happy and robust, with its roots deeply embedded in the shaly soil. Farther on, where deeper soil and more permanent water allowed, we found *Correa lawrenciana* in its uncommon bright red form. It is a graceful shrub with longish ovate leaves, and its pendant tubular flowers are displayed clearly.

In a slightly drier forest, not too far on, we discovered a patch of the unusual green-flowered mint bush, *Prostanthera walteri*. It was only 60 centimetres high, but scrambled up and over smaller plants to make a patch several metres long.

To cap off a great week we sought out and found in the forest areas south-east of Buchan the only Victorian stand of *Eucalyptus maculata,* the spotted gum. They grow in a limited area which has been declared a forest reserve, and are no doubt remnants of a once bigger population. Pressure from a changing climate, and from trees that have adapted better to this changing, now means that *Eucalyptus maculata* has only a tenuous hold in this area.

A great flock of wattle birds streaming overhead, calling in their characteristic, oddly musical way, told us that the spotted gums were for them a favourite haunt for food.

We stood for some time beneath the towering white trunks, with their familiar dimples and light-grey patches. To feel the presence of their strength and their ancient beauty was a fitting end to another Victorian discovery trip.

31 RAINFORESTS

NEW SOUTH WALES & QUEENSLAND

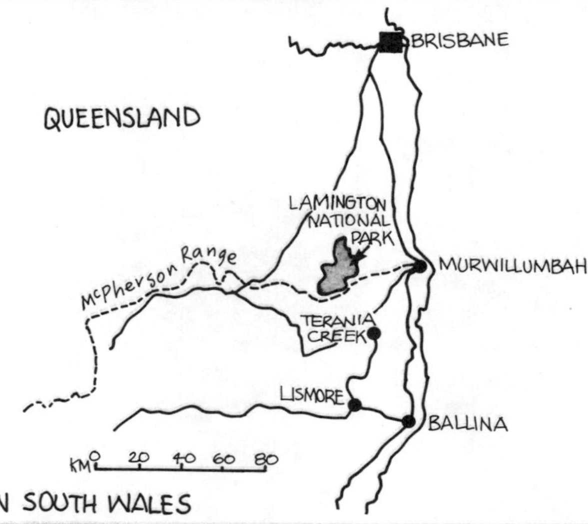

It is disconcerting, when you are accustomed to the woodlands or heathlands of the southern parts of the continent, to find yourself in an environment in which the components are hardly recognisable. I felt this strangeness when I had my first encounter with the rainforests on Lamington Plateau in Queensland.

We were spending a few days at the historic O'Reilly's Guest House at Lamington National Park, the home of the late Bernard O'Reilly, whose story of the epic rescue of the survivors of a plane crash in 1937 was standard reading for many post-war teenagers. Apart from experiencing such a complex area, I wished to look at plants that had potential for use indoors. The foliage and structure of many species, together with the fruit of some, suggested that there was a huge and barely tapped source of beautiful plants for both indoor and patio use. Doubtless many would be quite at home sharing a moist shaded area of a garden with ferns.

On the first day, we walked 16 kilometres – and there was hardly a tree that I could recognise with certainty. The main problem in attempting recognition was the height to which the trees grow. A stiff neck at the end of that day was a legacy of constant gazing up into distant foliage that crowned 30-50 metres of trunk. It was only by inspecting juvenile plants, few of which we could link with the giants above us, that some identification could be made. Many of those we finally managed to identify would eventually grow too large in a garden situation and would be considerably restricted in a small container. Yet they are so attractive just in foliage alone that they would provide many years of enjoyment.

A number of lilly-pillies – which include *Eugenia* and *Syzygium*, and in particular *Eugenia coolminiana* and *Eugenia leuhmannii* – could be grown just for their habit. Both have berries that are not only attractive but (in the case of *Eugenia coolminiana*) certainly edible. These are a bright pink and almost the size of the commercial cherry. They are treated as such in Queensland and are eaten as a dessert or made into jam.

Keith Williams's informative *Native Plants of Queensland* was seldom closed. Through that, I was able to identify *Eugenia leuhmannii*, atop of which masses of bright red berries could be seen. Like the previous species, it has shiny foliage complementing the lustre of the fruits. I already have this plant growing indoors hydroponically and it flowers and fruits regularly.

Two closely related plants, *Callicoma serratifolia* (which I did know well) and *Davidsonia pruriens* (to which I had my first introduction) would grace any indoor garden. I have often written of the first, which has lightly fur-covered, toothed foliage and ball heads of cream flowers. The second was a plant with a structure I had not encountered in an Australian plant. Leaves are pinnate, toothed and partially hairy, and are about 15 centimetres long; new growth is a delicate pink. They arise from a rhachis, or common leaf stem, which bears a broad fringe similar to the leaf structure, down the length of either side. The compound leaf is held almost horizontally, so that you look down onto the structure from above. Though there may be certain disadvantages in cleaning the lightly hairy foliage, I found its softness a pleasant contrast to the over-polished appearance of many indoor plants. An attractive flower is followed by an edible plum-like fruit. What more could one want?

The walking stick palm, *Linospadix monostachys*, was a common small plant to 1.5 metres wherever the floor of the rainforest was less dense. The fine trunks bore umbrella-like heads of gently arching leaves, and hanging down over these, like a long string of beads, are the orange berries. Evidently the plant was collected in great numbers during World War II, so that it could be made into walking sticks for injured soldiers. Today it serves a less functional, though more decorative, purpose, as a hardy container plant.

Above the waterfalls and on the creeks running steeply out of the forests, one plant tends to dominate in framing the falls and in lining the banks. I had known of *Helmholtzia acorifolia* for some years as an attractive tufted lily to a metre in height, but I was not prepared for the great clumps of strap leaves which, in places, were over 2 metres high. Of all the plants seen, only one carried the delicate heads of shell-pink flowers, held on fleshy deeper pink stems. These occasionally perfumed blooms, which open in late spring through to autumn, enhance the robust habit of the plant. As an indoor plant the size attained would more likely be a metre.

Bordering a few creeks, but not in the same profusion, is *Alocasia macrorrhiza*, which you could be forgiven for thinking was an escaped arum lily. It has the same soft broadly cordate leaves on fleshy stems and, though it was not in flower, remnant floral parts indicated that it had a similar spathe-like structure. Later experiences showed this to be so, and the flowers had a delicate pervasive perfume.

These were but a few of a multitude of plants we saw, and of which so little is known in southern states.

One lesson clearly learnt from this specialised environment is the importance of soil structure and nutrient. The floor of the forest is constantly covered with decaying leaves from which all plants draw their food needs. Early settlers made the mistake of assuming the soil was very fertile, and cleared vast areas – to discover that the land supported crops for only one season before it ran out of nutrient; and, since little was available artificially, it then fell into disuse. It was only the forest litter, which was renewed annually, that supplied the elements the plants required.

Without a doubt, the most impressive and largest trees on Lamington were *Nothofagus moorei*, the northern beech. Unlike the southern species, this one has a massive buttressed trunk (a structure shared by many rainforest trees) and large ovate crinkled leaves. We found one so huge that we were able to shelter from a sudden shower inside a rotted-out section of trunk.

Birds are not easy to see in these dense, dark forests, though their calls are frequently heard. Somewhat disconcerting if you have not had a previous initiation, is the call of a member of the bowerbird group. Its call sounds like the miaowing of a lost cat, and the name green catbird, could not be more apt. No doubt I wasn't the first person to spend some time prowling about under logs and bushes looking for a non-existent feral cat.

This heavily-built bird, about 30 centimetres from tip to tail, is a dull olive-green on the back and spotted beneath, which makes it extremely difficult to see. Its colouring and its roosting position in the rainforest trees make it almost impossible to locate, and it was only by sitting quietly for nearly an hour that we caught the slightest glimpse of one. The two other bowerbirds in the area, the satin and the regent, were much easier to see, since they were regular visitors to the O'Reilly's guesthouse.

The satin bowerbird is an intense blue-black with violet eyes, and the regent is black and bright yellow with yellow eyes. Both had bowers close by in the forest, with the usual collection of coloured objects lining the pathway into the bower.

We did not see any of these birds in the Terania Creek rainforests north of Lismore, in northern NSW; but we did see a new collection of plants, different from those at Lamington, and again the potential of many for horticultural use was evident. The lesser known small-to-medium trees, many with beautiful foliage, habit, or fruit, as well as flowers, would lend themselves well to either indoor or patio cultivation. Melbourne is behind Brisbane and Sydney in the use of plants for this form of decoration, but we are gradually recognising their aesthetic value.

One plant, *Geissois* (pronounced Geese-wha) *benthami* is grown both for its brilliant red new growth and its abundant foliage.

Jagera pseudorhus (named to suggest a similarity to Rhus) is superficially like that well-known garden plant. Its habit is umbrella-like, with the fine, pinnate foliage clothing the plant in soft layers.

The common names of lace flower and snow wood are applied to species of *Abarema*. *Abarema sapindoides*, like the other species, has ferny foliage and very showy powder-puff flowers. The initial colour is orange, fading with age to white. It is an ideal plant for both indoor and in open conditions where there is no threat of frost.

Flindersia maculata is the leopard wood of very dry areas of Australia. Most of this family, however, occurs in moister areas, and we saw species growing in the heart of the rainforest. *Flindersia xanthoxyla*, or yellow wood, is often referred to as a handsome tree. It is weeping in habit, with foliage that is boldly fern-like in appearance.

Many trees have fruit on which the resident bird populations feed. A number of these belong to the myrtle family, and include *Acmena*, *Syzygium* and *Rhodamnia*. One species of the last-mentioned, *Rhodamnia argentea*, stood out from the greens of the forest because of the intense grey texture, which was very obvious on the backs of leaves.

It is important to know the conditions required for successfully growing these plants indoors. Basically they need a sandy soil with high levels of humus, constant moisture without bogging, and an environment around the foliage both warm and moist. With plants indoors, most losses occur either because air conditioning desiccates the foliage, or dust and grime chokes it, or because there is not enough air and light. The plants should be regularly taken outside, where the foliage and soil can be thoroughly washed over and through with a hose.

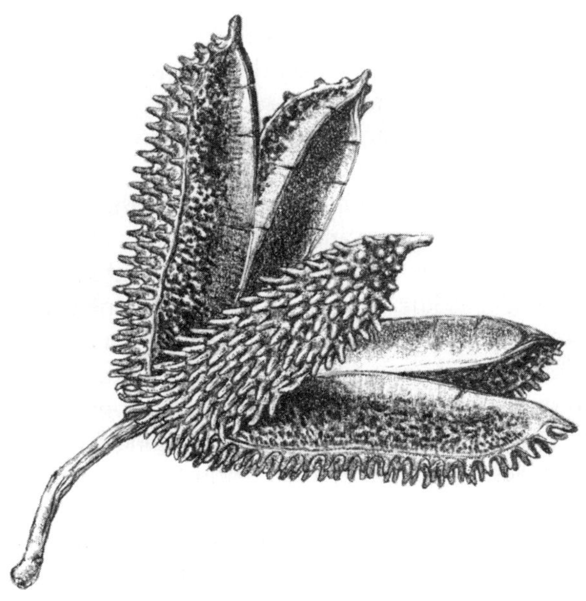

Flindersia maculata

32 COASTAL HEADLANDS

NEW SOUTH WALES

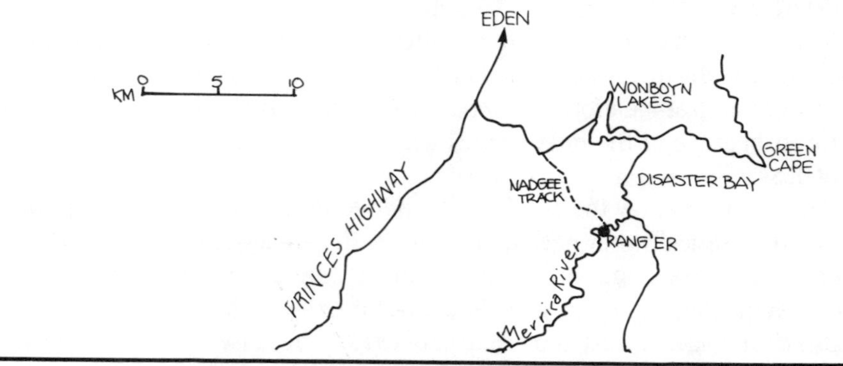

Plants of coastal headlands, where wind constantly assaults the vegetation, have developed floristic characteristics quite different from those of nearby forests, in which relatively normal development of habit is found. I have deliberately sought out areas where headlands carrying heathland flora are likely to occur, and seldom have I been disappointed with the interest and diversity these areas provide. The southern coastal areas of New South Wales have many such areas, and on each, and often only there, I have found plants which have become, or will become, hardy and attractive horticultural specimens.

Green Cape is one of the most southerly headlands jutting into the southern ocean. On its southern side are the broad waters and sweeping curves of Disaster Bay. The Green Cape lighthouse is still one of the important manned signalling points, many of which dot this long coastline. The approach to the cape is made from the Princes Highway south of Boydtown. The track winds through dense eucalypt forests with an under storey including a compact yellow flowering form of *Banksia spinulosa*, and two of our most graceful wattles, *Acacia cognata*, and the very similar *A. subporosa*. These two large shrubs have a weeping habit, and are smothered in soft lemon or yellow flowers in early spring.

Though both these plants occupy similar sites, usually in moister gullies or shaded areas, they can be readily distinguished by their leaves. *A. cognata* has a very fine leaf with one easily discernible midvein, whereas *A. subporosa* has broader leaves, with a number of parallel longitudinal veins, visible to the naked eye. The foliage and seed pods of the latter are quite sticky.

As one approaches the coast the plant communities change, owing to a dramatic change in the soil type. Instead of a gritty clay, we find ourselves on old deep sands, that cap underlying rock. Two trees dominate, one a eucalypt, the other the closely related *Angophora*. The eucalypt, *E. longifolia,* is found only in a long narrow coastal strip running to the Victorian border, and is a tall forest tree, with a stocking of bark, and large cream flowers in bundles of three. *Angophora floribunda,* also tall, has a spreading, open canopy, and is softly barked all over. At Salt Water Creek, farther north, it is found on coastal flats, providing a beautiful parkland setting for campers. This species just sneaks into Victoria as far as western Mallacoota, and is common in near coastal areas of New South Wales.

Angophoras are profuse flowerers, and flowering is accompanied by a rich nectar flow. This not only attracts bees and honeyeating birds, but also serves as a major part of the diet of small possums. Seldom is one fortunate enough to encounter the mouse-sized pygmy possum, so small and secretive is he. Since he is nocturnal and feeds high in a tree canopy, he is unlikely to be seen. It was then both a joy and a surprise to us one evening, camped under a grove of *Angophora,* to have one virtually drop into our laps.

It had obviously lost its footing (or tailing!) while either feeding or moving around the tree. Fortunately, it landed with a plop on our sloping tent fly, and then rolled to the ground. We saw a small movement out of the range of our lamplight and, thinking it was a baby bird, went to investigate. Instead, clinging to the uppermost tip of a new bracken fern frond, was this delightful creature, with big eyes and twitching nose and ears. Obviously a bit shaken by its fall, it perched for some minutes while we examined it by torchlight. We did not wish to terrify it; but feeling that it would be safer in the tree I proffered a finger as a mode of transport, and received a sharp nip – whereupon it jumped from the bracken and disappeared towards the base of the tree.

This little fellow is known as *Cercartetus nanus,* and has a Western Australian counterpart in *C. concinnus,* which is also found on Kangaroo Island.

I have been sidetracked in describing the way to Green Cape, but it is an area of such interest that even when you are actually travelling through it, and not just writing about it, similar diversions lead you away.

The heathland section of the cape opens out dramatically from the forest, and whereas one minute you are driving through *Banksia serrata* 5–8 metres tall, the next it scarcely reaches knee height. This part of the cape receives the full force of wind from three directions as it slopes gradually to the north, east and south. Only in sheltered hollows does any plant attain large shrub proportions and it is often a low tangled network of branches. Even the two stringybark eucalypts, *E. obliqua* and *E. muellerana,* both of which farther inland are trees of large proportion, are seldom more than gnarled shrubs.

Two 'oddities', or so I called them because I did not expect to find them here, were *Acacia terminalis* and *Crowea exalata,* both atypical of their normal habit. The wattle, with its soft multi-coloured ferny foliage and glowing flowers was growing as an under shrub, whereas normally, throughout east Gippsland forests, it is an open shrub to 3 metres. The *Crowea,* which is a small shrub found from alpine to mallee fringe habitats, was a mound a few centimetres high, dotted with its familiar waxy pink flowers.

The amount of flower and nectar being produced by *Banksia serrata*, and the beauty and size of the yellow and grey flowers not being diminished by this modifying environment, led us to wonder whether the pygmy possum also ventured here.

We could not answer this question, but we did on this and subsequent trips, with much stealth and patience, catch glimpses of the elusive ground parrot. This shy bird moves at a low level and then only over short distances. It is such a distinctive colour – bright green with irregular, black and yellow markings – that you require only a glimpse to make a positive identification.

No doubt I had disturbed this one as I moved through the heathland, and it flew low and quickly to ground close to where Sue had been standing motionless for some time. We sighted it twice more, but only fleetingly during more than an hour. It is listed as uncommon, but I would wonder whether its rarity is perhaps more an indication of the difficulty in sighting it. It was obviously in a perfect habitat, since many seed-bearing plants grew in this tangle of vegetation; and *Hakea* and *Bossiaea*, as well as the *Acacia* species, were a constant source of food.

Farther north, and just south of Ulladulla, is a small rocky headland known as Schnapper Point, a possible indication of its major attraction. There is little soil here, but this has not deterred several plants from establishing small colonies. The dwarf form of *Banksia spinulosa*, which is common in the forests, was reduced to a bonsai plant. Even so, it evidently flowered successfully, judging by the bleached seed capsules. Beside it grew *Melaleuca hypericifolia*, also common at Ulladulla, but more frequently found on the tablelands, and north of Sydney on sandstone plateaux. Like the *Banksia*, this shrub, which has attractive lustrous red brushes, and normally grows to between 2 and 3 metres, was a low compact mound. It is certainly the most extreme situation I have seen either species inhabiting, and illustrates their toughness and versatility.

In the more sheltered heathland behind Schnapper Point we saw the shy emu-wren; so named because of its fine tail feathers. It is a pretty bird with sparrow-like colouring, but with blue being the dominant frontal colour. The fine tail is by far the longest part of this secretive little bird.

While we were camped farther south toward Bateman's Bay, we had an amusing experience. Again we were among *Angophora floribunda* and, having returned from a swim, we were relaxing on woven lounge chairs. Unbeknown to us a lace monitor, or goanna, had crept into our camp looking for food. He had moved under Sue's lounge, and evidently a salty under-thigh appealed to his taste. Needless to say Sue leapt up when she felt the rough strokes on her legs through the webbing; and the goanna, seeing his lunch disappearing, took fright and made straight for the nearest tree, which he climbed to a safe height then peered down at us.

Goannas scavenge refuse as well as raiding nests for eggs or young birds; and no doubt possums or mice, and even smaller lizards, become their victims. Perfectly harmless, they are very much a part of these coastal forests, and even seem at home walking along the edge of the breakers collecting whatever the waves may wash ashore.

33 POSTSCRIPT

One day, after wading through page after page of my abominable longhand, my very tolerant and intelligent typist, Julie, said, 'How do you remember all this? You just seem to sit down and write.' I had never thought about it, and simply answered that, having had such experiences and taken a few notes, I remembered the detail many years later. I also said to Julie that the desire to investigate was the essence, together with the wish to learn and the readiness to go anywhere to gain first-hand experience.

It is not enough just to move through the continent without understanding what you are looking at. And we must seek answers to things we observe that may appear a paradox: limestone caves at Buchan, in high country 100 kilometres from the sea; a particular plant with populations 2000 kilometres apart; the imprint of a fossil of a plant now extinct in this part of the world, embedded in a block of stone; a spider that carries bubbles of air on its legs beneath the water.

Why do I consider this learning so important? Not only because it is interesting, but because a knowledge of the history and complexity of this land brings a respectful understanding, whereas a lack of it breeds indifference or even hostility.

One can excuse early pioneers for the mistakes they made in clearing trees excessively. But that even now, areas such as Queensland's Daintree rainforests are being threatened is not only inexcusable, in view of our experience and knowledge, but a national and international crime.

We have the wrong sorts of people in positions of power, people without knowledge or vision whose decisions are prompted by opportunism or short-term vested local interest and apathetically condoned. State and Federal boundaries were designed for convenience of management and do not give the Governments of the day an inalienable right to do what they wish within these imaginary boundaries. Australia's indigenous people developed a harmony with the land, which evolved into a spirituality; and if we can believe the latest finding, that they have been on this continent for at least 150 000 years, we can start to appreciate the intensity of this spirituality. Our modern philosophies pale beside this time span, and few of us understand the loss this race must feel.

Sadly, I see that, unless we as a nation dramatically alter our attitudes, unless we, too, develop a philosophy of reverence and a nurturing understanding of this land, it will exact retribution in full. We have done our worst in two hundred years to clear the land of Aborigines, by poison, disease, and alienation of their spirituality, just as we have and are still doing our worst to modify the land to a point of no return.

In spite of all this I feel some optimism. A new order with an empathy to the environment is arising. It will not emerge overnight, and the battles will still be fought; some won, some lost. Shorter working hours mean greater leisure time; and as more people use this time constructively, they will, I hope, make bush journeys and see their country with open eyes and minds. And, of course, many will journey to areas I have not visited. In *Bush Journeys* there is a strong emphasis on heathland and drier sclerophyll forest; this is no accident. I have not written about the Flinders Ranges, because I have not been there; nor have I visited Ayers Rock; and the lusher islands off the Queensland coast are experiences which also still await me.

If there is a *Bush Journeys*, part 2, no doubt it will include some of these, and many less familiar places for which there was not room in this volume. On this warm spring morning, I sit writing with the light playing through the bright red new tips of a eucalyptus sapling. The grey thrush, the cuckoo, and the wattle bird are welcoming the warmth as a sign for them to recommence their breeding cycles; the grebes, coots, and moorhens are busily feeding and nest-building on my lake. And I am certain of one thing: the importance of these activities and cycles, and the importance of preserving an environment where these magical processes can survive.

By the same author:

NATIVE GARDENS
by Bill Molyneux and Ross Macdonald

Native Gardens shows how to create a natural bush landscape around your home. The authors present hundreds of landscaping ideas in practical, step-by-step illustrations and photographs which will enable you to make an attractive, low-maintenance garden suitable for all your recreational needs and for our long, hot summers.

Good gardens with minimal maintenance seldom happen by accident. Using this book you can learn how to assess your needs and draw simple plans; prepare the soil, place rocks and choose the right plants for your landscape.

You can simulate the textures and scents of the bush by using Australian plants with rocks, sand, gravel and bush litter, or give an established garden new life by integrating some of our native plants with existing exotic trees and shrubs. Create the illusion of space with clever planting in even the smallest inner-city garden. Discover which plants complement seating, terraces, pool or utility areas and driveways.

The creative and unusual ideas in this book even show you how to have an attractive lawn and nature strip without using a lawn-mower.

FOREST TREES OF AUSTRALIA
by Douglas Boland et. al.

Forest Trees of Australia describes and illustrates 223 of our most important native trees, selected because of their environmental significance, their importance to the timber industry, or because they are conspicuous in the landscape.

One hundred and thirty-seven eucalypt and 86 non-eucalypt species, including the more important rainforest ones, are extensively described and illustrated. Brief ecological information is also given. Where a range of species occurs throughout Australia, such as in a large genus like *Melaleuca,* the main species from most Australian states have been included.

Since the first edition of *Forest Trees of Australia* appeared in 1957, it has become a standard reference, both locally and overseas, on the main indigenous trees in this country. New maps, photographs and illustrations show us a wonderfully diverse range of forests, from mangrove swamps, monsoon regions and deserts, to alpine areas, and majestic stands of temperate rainforest.

Forest Trees of Australia is an essential reference, an unsurpassed guide to identification, for horticulturists, botanists, foresters, students, farmers, and all those who are interested in our native trees.

TROPICAL ORCHIDS OF AUSTRALIA
by P. S. Lavarack and B. Gray

Tropical Orchids of Australia discusses about 230 species which grow in habitats as diverse as hot paperbark woodlands and cool misty rainforests. For the first time the known facts and accepted theories on habitats, ecology, origins, conservation and taxonomy are drawn together. Many new species are fully described and illustrated in fine black and white plates.

Habitat information is used to develop suggestions on how to cultivate tropical orchids successfully; the information is also presented in a comprehensive chart never before attempted in an Australian publication. Twenty-five choice orchids well worth cultivating (each illustrated in colour) are dealt with in detail: these range from the well-known *Dendrobium bigibbum* (the Cooktown Orchid) and the striking *Phalaenopsis amabilis* to the rarer *Bulbophyllum longiflorum.* Other chapters cover natural hybrids, classification, name changes and National Parks where tropical orchids may be found, making this the most authoritative and up-to-date book available on our indigenous tropical orchids. Over eighty magnificent colour plates display their significant horticultural potential and amazing diversity of form, size and colour. *With a foreword by Dr Phillip Cribb, Royal Botanic Gardens, Kew, England.*